Writing for Business

Mary C. Bromage

Writing for Business

Ann Arbor Paperbacks
The University of Michigan Press

First edition as an Ann Arbor Paperback 1965

Library of Congress Catalog Card No. 65-21770
Published in the United States of America by
The University of Michigan Press and simultaneously
in Toronto, Canada, by Ambassador Books Limited
Manufactured in the United States of America

Book Design by Quentin Fiore

Preface

Any acknowledgment of help in preparing this book is due chiefly to businessmen themselves. In working with members of various firms, I found out quickly that businessmen are ready to recognize communication as a special art and ready to recognize its subtleties and difficulties.

From groups including finance specialists, engineers, accountants, lawyers, and utility executives meeting over the past few years in seminars has come an abundance of ideas and data. The selection of material I present here is intended for others engaged in writing on the job, and for university students who, before long, will be joining business organizations.

Permission to quote illustrative passages has been kindly granted by these publishers: Houghton Mifflin Company for Winston S. Churchill's *The Second World War;* Random House, Inc. for William Faulkner's *Intruder in the Dust* (copyright 1948); Simon and Schuster, Inc. for Sloan Wilson's *Man in the Gray Flannel Suit* (copyright 1955); The Viking Press, Inc. for *The Portable Mark Twain* edited by Bernard de Voto (copyright 1946); McGraw-Hill Book Company for Mark Schorer's *Sinclair Lewis: An American Life* (copyright© 1961); Yale University Press for Charles L. Stevenson's *Ethics and Language; The New York Times;* and *The Detroit Free Press.* Permission was also given for the use of the author's own material which previously appeared in the *Michigan Business Review* at The University of Michigan and in the *Journal of Accountancy.*

The relationship of illustrations drawn from literary masterpieces, old and new, to "bread and butter" writing needs little justification. Writing, whether for business or pleasure, deals in certain commodities (the word, the sentence, and the paragraph) and has certain aims: arousing interest, communicating expeditiously, convincing the reader. To call some writing creative and some not is a fallacy, for the merest scrawl on a telephone note pad is intended to create some effect upon its recipient. An impression of the communicator, as well as of the content, is produced upon the reader's mind.

In quoting the words of writers and leaders in business, in government, and in academic life, individual authorization was received from Robert P. Briggs, Consumers' Power Company; Courtney C. Brown, Columbia University; George H. Brown, Ford Motor Company; Fred C. Foy, Koppers Company, Inc.; George Gribbin, Young and Rubicam, Inc.; John Hersey, author; Raymond Kendall, Itek Laboratories; Alfred Rice, trustee; G. Marion Sadler, American Airlines; J. A. Spencer, General Electric Company; Philip Sporn, American Electric Power Service Corporation; James J. Sweeney, Museum of Fine Arts, Houston, Texas; Stewart L. Udall, U.S. Department of the Interior; Thomas J. Watson, Jr., International Business Machines Corporation; E. B. White, *The New Yorker;* Theodore O. Yntema, Ford Motor Company. The Clements Library of The University of Michigan gave permission for use of a letter written by its late director, Dr. Randolph G. Adams. The Civil Service Commission of Nassau County, New York, and the tradesmen of the Meadowbrook Hospital willingly supplied certain information.

Source material for the study of functional writing grows everywhere that offices and plants are found. Growing apace is the demand for improvement in the recording and transmitting of ideas, information, and decisions. Most often this demand originates from top management.

Although different businesses deal in different processes and products, they hold language in common. Insofar as paperwork is concerned, they are working with the same tools as those of professional authors. Where writing is at stake, why not look for models to those who are the professionals? Why not look among the really great? Churchill provides one such model, that of a man writing under pressure.

No miracle can be turned by or for those facing up to the demands for written communications. Much can, however, be accomplished to clarify the results when the professions of business and writing join forces. This book is not intended to take the place of, but to be used in conjunction with manuals of grammatical rules and references. I have not tried to lay down laws, to prescribe cures, or to formulate "good" writing.

My undertaking here is to show possibilities for expeditious writing and to point out the choices a writer must make knowingly to deliver his message with maximum impact.

M.C.B.

Contents

3: Managing Sentences and Paragraphs 40

4: Planning Form 59

I: Mastering Communication

The fashionable term for something as old as the worlds of public and private affairs themselves is communication. Both worlds depend upon leadership and understanding. The difference today lies in the dilation of the field of managerial operations. The modern executive, relying more and more on the typed or telephoned word to convey his business, may long for some new magic. If the magic of communicating is going to be made to work, it will not be by magicians but by practitioners.

Recognizing Objectives

The individual who is required to submit something in writing, whether it is an estimate of plant capacity for purposes of expansion or a manual of job procedures, is fortunate. The task ahead of him is simple compared to that of the writer of fiction, for the businessman, unlike the novelist, has a ready-made subject and a ready-made reader. The inseparability of thinking and writing is our first lesson. To think well off paper means to communicate well on paper. Nice distinctions must be drawn between generalized assertions and supportive data—between merely informing and issuing judgments, between causes and effects. Logic is the marrow of the bone.

Thinking must be free. If an individual owned nothing else, his thoughts would remain his indisputably, communicated or uncommunicated. To stultify mental initiative and impose one way of thinking is to put an end forever to its value. Under dictatorships the output of fiction and non-fiction dwindles and professional authors take to translating as their only safe work. The thought process in a free economy must be daring; in transfer to others thought must be represented fairly and winningly.

Free, inventive, and creative as the individual's habit of mind has to be, he must measure his success with language by definite criteria. In business there are two: profit and good will. The profit in a commercial or industrial venture must, of course, be monetary if the enterprise is to survive, but the word profit carries other increments. Henry Ford wanted to produce a car which the millions could afford. Profits connote more than dollars with the leaders of business. The good of mankind plays its part in an economy built on its own kind of idealism.

Good will in a free society is essential in the producer-consumer relationship. Without good will profits fly out the window. When the housewife can take her pick from a dozen stores, she will shop where she likes not only the price but the attitude. Though the customer may not always be right, the seller who puts the customer in the wrong may reap a short-range profit only. Personalized messages, the informal but dignified approach, the affirmative, encouraging assurance—these are means of good will expressed face to face and on paper.

Writing which focuses on the dual objective of profit and good will is businesslike writing. The definition is as broad as the mind of the executive makes it. But once we define our particular utilization of the written language, we realize that we must wield the same tools as all other writers, professional or nonprofessional: words and forms and sequences. Writing is as much a skill as constructing bridges, designing accounting systems, or producing cars. Whereas few authors try to build a bridge, audit an account, or produce a car, most engineers, accountants, and automotive manufacturers write voluminously. To do so profitably, they should look to the masters. To write successfully requires that you read selectively and well. Writing and reading are the two sides of the coin of communication.

Dovetailing words to a purpose is a skill few have practiced in business or in politics with the success of Sir

Winston Churchill. He was a master practitioner. His writing was less for pleasure than, in his youth, for profit, and after that, for public purpose. What seems in his words like magic is no secret he kept up his sleeve.

Sir Winston made language one of his means to power and influence. "The man who could not say what he had to say in good English," he declared, "could not have very much to say that was worth listening to at all." And he made a point of drafting his own letters and reports himself. "Good English" for him came to mean accuracy, brevity, and the right emotional tone.

"An efficient and a successful administration manifests itself equally in small as in great matters," he wrote to General Ismay in 1943, commenting on the code name "Triumphant" proposed for an operational plan. Words smacking of boastfulness, such as "Triumphant," had no place where lives were at stake, he admonished; nor did anything indicative of despondency like "Woebetide" or "Jumble." Terms frivolous in character like "Bunnyhug" or "Ballyhoo" he cited as even less suitable, so he wound up what amounted to a directive on code names with the order that none be approved till he saw them. If the choice of the right word was a small matter, it was nonetheless important.

Being Right and Brief

In the name of accuracy Churchill exercised constant vigilance. At the height of the Battle of the Atlantic he insisted that "Iceland" be followed by a capital C—"Iceland (C)"—to distinguish it from Ireland. Every phrase he dictated got the greatest care, according to his secretary, to prevent misinterpretation. There was no limit to the retyping for the sake of accuracy alone.

Brevity ranked next with him. Brevity coupled with accuracy called for the utmost selectivity. In 1941 he wrote to General Ismay: "Let me have a time-table (on one sheet of paper) of what the Navy will do on each day from the 'Alert' on Day 1 to Day 20, and what forces will be in hand." Such precision could not be achieved without effort, he knew, and he did not begrudge the hours he spent himself. When he dictated, his secretary had to keep track of the number of words, for he was likely to stop and demand to know how many at any moment.

His impatience with verbosity boiled over when it came to telegrams. "You spoke to me the other day," he replied to his Foreign Affairs Minister early in the war, "about the length of telegrams. I think that this is an evil which ought to be checked. Ministers and Ambassadors abroad seem to think that the bigger the volume of their reports home, the better is their task discharged. . . . It is sheer laziness not compressing thought into a reasonable space."

Getting the Feel

While he was striving for accuracy and brevity, he was also employing subtler arts in his letters, directives, reports, and speeches. Imparting information was seldom the sole objective of his carefully chosen words, his studied sentences, and his ordered paragraphs. Paragraphs had to fit on one another neatly. The rousing of his readers or listeners to some greater effort usually lay close to the surface of whatever he had to say.

His sensitivity to the emotional implication of the lowest linguistic denominator, the word, often moved him to rebuke. At a staff conference in Downing Street, as Dwight D. Eisenhower recalls, a young officer innocently used the word "bodies" in referring to the number of soldiers needed for a particular mission. Churchill interrupted with an impassioned outburst against talking in cold blood of soldiers as if they were merely corpses.

His fastidiousness about words was nothing new. Some twenty years earlier the House of Commons, debating a document he had helped prepare, quibbled over its use of the word "treaty" for something being signed by His Majesty's Government with a would-be-independent Ireland. The objection was that treaties were signed only between sovereign nations. Churchill rose in remonstrance over the quibble to defend the wording: "When you come to choose the words you will use, and when your actual position is not affected thereby, you should surely use the words most likely to help you to secure the goodwill, support, and agreement which you seek."

When it came to naming Britain's civil defense force in World War II, he did not think much of the uninspiring title, "Local Defense Volunteers." Someone then proposed "Civic Guard" but he held out for "Home Guard." This, he said, sounded much more "compulsive."

Writing to Fit Time and Place

One-syllable, concrete words like "home" and "guard" came to drown out his own peacetime habit of polysyllabification. Everyone remembers the wartime Prime Minister's businesslike simplicity of: "Give us the tools and we will finish the job." He is even more famous for the thirty-three words: ". . . we shall fight on the beaches, we shall fight on the landing grounds, we shall fight in the fields and on the streets, we shall fight in the hills; we shall never surrender." All but three of these words are of one syllable, and all are action or name words used with the first-person pronoun. A less familiar description of the war from the same pen is this: ". . . the actual conflict had to be more like one ruffian bashing the other on the snout with a club, a hammer, or something better." His figures of speech are unmistakable as to image and impact.

By sentence pattern as well as word choice are his effects achieved. There is no one Churchillian sentence style. As the purpose altered, so did the approach. His earlier peacetime rhetoric was rotund and empurpled. Once, when a young man, he was forced to own up to what he admitted were "terminological inexactitudes." As times changed, so did he and so did his manner of speaking and writing.

The clipped, cutoff style came later in his life. As the press of affairs grew heavier upon him, he wrote tersely and pointedly, stripping down his old Victorian superstructure. The most communicative words convey feeling as well as fact, and the writer who feels keenly shapes words to accord with his time and place. The mid-twentieth-century left no time for words for words' sake. It was a time for action.

It is the very variety—the adaptation of structure to the purpose in hand—that is Churchillian. His style underwent conspicuous change. But he could never resist the quick jab, not even in the fearful days of 1940: "Here in London which Herr Hitler says he will reduce to ashes . . . we are waiting for the long-promised invasion. So are the fishes." His sentences can lift the chin or drag on the feet; they can pat the back or deliver a body blow. For swift movement, it is hard to equal this statement: "Never in the field of human conflict was so much owed by so many to so few." Here, the triple series builds a swift climax to the final emphasis, strategically withheld until the last word. Another staccato message was conveyed by three short, simple, declarative sentences: "I have some news for the House. It is good news. The Royal Navy has struck a crippling blow at the Italian Fleet."

For lengthier passages, affirmative declarations are interspersed with questions. All the devices of parallel phraseology, alliteration, and climactic emphasis were employed in his crucial letter to the French leader, Reynaud, dated June 13, 1940: "We renew to the French Republic our pledge and resolve to continue the struggle at all costs in France, in this island, upon the oceans, and in the air, wherever it may lead us, using all our resources to the utmost limit and sharing together the burden of repairing the ravages of war."

Practical application of the English language to executive communications, whether in politics or business, is not a new world to conquer. It does not offer the executive any miracle solutions. Once beyond the ABC's of writing there is no primer, only precedent and practice.

For precedent, Sir Winston Churchill—in his time journalist, novelist, biographer, historian, editor, essayist, speech writer—offers on any one page a dozen lessons. He himself learned painfully to write and never worked for letter perfection in rules of grammar. He grew with the times, and his words were shaped to fit them. His own comment in a different connection might be taken to heart by the hesitant writer: "The maxim 'Nothing avails but perfection' may be spelt shorter: 'Paralysis.'" His pen has proved mightier than many another kind of weapon in the management of great undertakings. Its mightiness lay in the universal virtues of good English: accuracy, brevity, human tone.

Today, every businessman has to write and to read increasing amounts of paperwork. Few businessmen feel that they are able to do either easily. "Everyone finds some part of his job more difficult than other parts," one systems analyst commented. "In my work, I am required to write a report after each project is completed. While I enjoy completing each project, I find it difficult to write a report."

Because of the decentralization of corporations and the specialization of skills, there is more and more to write on the job. At the same time, there is less and less time to read. From these counterpressures comes the feeling, when you sit down with pen, pencil, or dictaphone in hand, of being unable to communicate all you have to say within the built-in limits of the situation.

One piece of good fortune is yours. Not only do you *have* to write (someone wants a fact, someone wants an idea, someone wants an analysis), you have to write on a deadline. In writing, a deadline is the kindest thing. Otherwise, pencils may be sharpened, the desk cleared, calls held, but the difficulty of reducing your ideas to paper will make you prey to all possible distractions, postponements, avoidances. Fred C. Foy, Chairman of the Board, Koppers Company, Inc., puts it this way:

> One of the greatest weaknesses in our executives at all levels is their utter inability to state clearly and understandably in writing the nature of a business problem, what they want to do about it, and why.

Writing will become easier if it becomes a habit. The rising demand for reports and letters—the whole battery of business communications—makes writing a businessman's business. If you want to get the habit, choose surroundings where you can sit still, whether alone or in the hubbub. Even your choice of pencil may aid and abet your work. Paper—the kind you like to cover, lined or unlined—is worth taking into account. Don't, at first, try to write for long at a stretch. You might start working by your watch till you can increase your span. Some professional writers set themselves stints. Ernest Hemingway, for instance, got up to write every morning before daylight at his Idaho home because he liked to hunt and fish in the afternoons.

Proceeding Step by Step

The businessman usually knows what he is going to write without waiting for the inspiration on which the novelist, the poet, or the dramatist depends. It is much easier to tackle a specific assignment within a specific time limit. Such a situation usually develops step by step.

Getting the Request

First comes the phone call: "Write me a report on . . ." The voice names anything from multiple sourcing of automotive parts to construction of a new power plant. The request—formally speaking, the authorization—is ideally but infrequently clear-cut. Just what is wanted may not be resolved in the mind of the person who wants it. He may only know that, in a bothersome way, some problem has cropped up. You, upon being asked for a report, have to figure out what the problem is.

"Let me have," Prime Minister Winston Churchill would write during World War II to his Minister of Shipping, "on one sheet of paper the mainheads of your programme as at present settled of imports (a) in the next four months, (b) for the year 1941. I should be glad to have this during tomorrow (Saturday)."

Limiting the Subject

You are faced with defining your subject. Try to repeat in one sentence just what it is you are going to discuss. Setting the limits is essential, since you are not going to undertake an encyclopedia. If you whittle down the topic, much of your reader's work as well as your own is done. Defining the subject means putting your finger on what is wanted. In doing so, decide what you can safely put aside, whether the request spells out the limits or not. To get the report "in the bag," the drawstrings must be pulled tight. Churchill made his assignments for his colleagues easier when he built limits into his directives. Often, the circumscribing is left up to the writer.

Settling the Purpose

Once you have nicely defined the subject, you need to be clear on why there has to be a report on it in the first place —on the purpose, that is. Are you supposed to give information only? Or are you to give your ideas, opinions, recommendations for action? Obviously, Britain's Minister of Shipping in replying would have been out of order, that Saturday, to suggest an increase or decrease in the imports established for the given periods. What his chief wanted was information only.

In business, as the chief's own decisions proliferate, more and more he is passing down the line the call for recommendations; he seeks increasingly to find his course of action in the advice of those upon whom he can rely. After all, people are hired because they can think. There is something to the old saying: "A penny for your thoughts." Churchill himself, as often as not, would leave his request wide open. "What," he demanded from his Director of Naval Intelligence at the beginning of the war, "is the position on the west coast of Ireland? Are there any signs of succouring U-boats in Irish creeks or inlets? It would seem that money should be spent to secure a trustworthy body of Irish agents to keep most vigilant watch. Has this been done? Please report."

In business, competence in specialized fields like marketing, accounting, production usually pervades the messages that flow back and forth. Such specialized competences, in fact, are the predominant characteristics of the letters and reports of successful businessmen. They are, from the word Go, subject-oriented. Less noticeable is an awareness of the readers. Except in the field of advertising, where the customer is not only right but king, the man on the receiving end of a business missive gets insufficient recognition. The clichés directed at him at the beginning and end of letters betray this weakness in the writer's imagination, in his willingness to turn, for a moment at least, from his technical subject matter, to talk specifically to his reader in terms of that individual's interests and needs. In settling the purpose of a communication, the writer needs to consider the reader as well as the material that will go into his message.

Gathering Data

Next, of course, comes the actual collecting of the material. If the report is for the purpose of informing only, your time will go primarily into accumulating facts. And when you are going to propose some decision, the facts are no less essential. Your sources are your own discovery: books and journals perhaps, but observations from the office, the assembly line, the laboratory, the market place are among other sources in business. Questionnaires, interviews, files, back records, balance sheets, trial runs may provide your data.

Whatever the source, recording the data accurately and fully is essential. You will assemble more material than you will incorporate, undoubtedly. Picking and choosing what is pertinent depends on you. Cards are a flexible device because they can be shuffled. Cards have another advantage: they automatically control the amount of note taking. Evidence, for such it will be in your report, must be traceable and authenticated. You do not want to bury your tracks. Don't ask your reader to take things on your word alone. That is throwing yourself on his mercy, and readers are not merciful.

Organizing Sequence

Once you have your material, you will start organizing it to meet the purpose you have pinpointed. Intuitive perceptions have by now begun occurring to you. Let your mind freewheel. The hardest part of the work is under way. Many people accomplish more in solitary thought than in collective sessions of "brain storming."

However your intuition asserts itself, you should take

note of your hunches. As Professor Jerome S. Bruner, Harvard psychologist, says: "The shrewd guess, the fertile hypothesis, the courageous leap to a tentative conclusion—these are the most valuable coin of the thinker at work, whatever his line of work."

You will be thinking the problem over when off the job. How do the angles fit together? Organization implies having a logical beginning, a middle, and an end. It is an imaginative affair. In the sequence of your facts will lie their clarity and appeal. Out of chaos you can create order, but it calls for plenty of forethought. In this phase, when you are mulling it over, real creativity is possible. A sequence may occasionally be prescribed for you. It makes the report easier to write; you can't go astray, but it gives you less opportunity.

In shaping a piece of written work, an outline provides a natural guide. After listing the introduction, jot down phrases for the main divisions into which the material you have gathered seems to fall. Some balance, though not strict equality, should emerge as to the significance and length of the sections. Here is where subheads will suggest themselves to you and may show whether you are lumping too much under one main heading. Of course, it is the arrangement of the several major divisions—sections or chapters—that will or will not lead your reader logically to the end section.

Your scheme of organization, in other words, should pay off as a result of outlining. As you progress, keep yourself free to change the sequence, to shift sections, to add and subtract. You will see new connections and natural transitions as you shuffle your cards. But do not make changes at random; plan with purpose aforethought. Systematic outlining relies on the use of standard symbols: Roman numerals for the major topics, capital letters for the second level of headings, Arabic numerals for the subheads, and then small letters.

For the meticulous thinker, large topics are capable of an indefinite number of divisions. As any topic that is divided will have two or more parts, at least two capital letters are needed if the Roman numeral heading is to be divided at all, and so down the line. A good outline should make sense if read through by the major headings, and the outline for each Roman numeral section should make sense if read in and of itself. Words which have to be repeated at several sublevels might better be transferred upward for economy's sake, so that they will appear only once at the spanning position. The value in outlining lies not in the niceties of the game, but in the inherent strengths or weaknesses revealed by the relationships such a system imposes on your thoughts. Unity or disparity will stand forth for what it is.

James Johnson Sweeney, when director of New York's Guggenheim Museum, said in discussing composition in painting that there is no such thing as "the happy accident." Composition in writing comes about the same way; it arises from plan or concept, but the plan needs to remain subject to change.

Choosing Format

From here on you should be in the swing of your material. The writing habit now begins to take over for you. It makes the next step easier. What you want to do now is to design the format for your report to fit your organizational scheme.

Familiarity with the form used is an advantage to writer and reader. In a given company, for instance, the color of the paper itself may signal the level from which a document emanates. At the Ford Motor Company, a "blue letter" is one that comes from top executive officers. By putting fresh ideas into a well-known and instantly identifiable frame of reference, the writer helps the reader get off to a better start.

Mere familiarity should not preclude the other advantage form can have: flexibility. Nothing gets out of date and nonfunctional faster than rigid forms. Purposes and channels and the very means of communication change. So should form. As a case in point, consider the annual report, once not much more than a financial statement, now more like a glossy magazine. The way a document looks should subserve the way it reads. The most colorful cover and the most elegant typography do not make incoherence coherent or turn confusion into order. Form for form's sake defeats itself.

You will be wise to adopt a standardized format if, in so doing, it will more truly reflect the nature of your message. The letter form, as a simple illustration, is currently demonstrating its flexibility. Sometimes, its salutation and complimentary close are dropped. In another variation of the stock pattern, the name and address of the recipient do not appear in the customary place above the salutation but at the lower left, after the signature. The impression of personal correspondence results when there is less above the message to impede direct contact. Interestingly enough, senior executives are not only sending letters in this style, but many are using smaller sheets of paper.

Report writers have a well-stocked armory of devices on which to draw. The format may include everything from embossed cover and title page to graphic art, as in the annual reports of great corporations. On the other hand, the format may be in the plain black and white that serves so many purposes at so little cost.

Drafting

The actual writing is like putting clothes on the form which you have set up. Your words constitute the style in which you dress your presentation. You may try various ways of expressing your facts and ideas. Are you going to use the personal pronoun or do you wish to speak impersonally? Are you going to use a technical vocabulary or remain on general terms with your reader? Do you need to exercise persuasion or to preserve total objectivity?

At this stage you are drafting, and drafting goes best if it goes fast. Unless a report is especially long, drafting it all at once will show you whether it hangs together. Once it is down on paper, let the draft stand at least overnight. Next day, you will "hear" how it sounds; you will be more likely to pick up errors of fact, judgment, or expression; you will be bored where your reader would be bored, confused where he would be, enlightened and convinced in other spots. You've often heard the saying that the way to revise is to cut. A blue pencil is as much help to a writer as a black one.

Revising

Revision may be superficial, affecting matters of style only, or it may be radical, tearing your work down to the roots, redefining and reorganizing your subject. Though not as difficult as the earlier stages of report writing, revision takes time—as much time, often, as you have, since writing is seldom perfected.

Maybe you will want to submit the preliminary version to coworkers for their comment. But don't enjoy this part of your job too long; paralysis can set in.

In some firms, senior members routinely review the work of juniors. This is the practice where the name appended to the communication is not that of the writer but is the name of a higher executive or of the firm itself. Outlines are sometimes submitted to a reviewer as the first step. Helpful changes resulting from a preliminary review may eliminate errors of fact, of structure, of emphasis, even of punctuation or spelling. Such changes, if explained, will help the original writer improve his writing. If the changes are not explained, the reviewer may expect his own time-consuming process of revision to continue indefinitely.

Another kind of alteration is sometimes made which, even when shown to the drafter, does not convince him. Such changes are based on stylistic prejudices of the senior and nothing more. One vice-president, for instance, disliked sentences beginning with a dependent clause and would automatically blue-pencil all such passages. Another reviewer was a stickler for certain, largely forgotten rules controlling "since" and "while." He blue-penciled a report in which the word "since" was used causatively:

> Since the budgeted figure was exceeded, an additional allocation had to be requested.

Although the sense of the offending word is obviously "because," the writer was directed to make the substitution and reserve "since" for references to time, as in the sentence:

> Since the first of the year, the budget had been exceeded.

Another peccadillo relates to the use of "while" in place of "although":

> While the budget was carefully considered, it did not prove adequate.

According to the purists, the word "although" should be substituted for "while," which should be used only to refer to time:

> While the budget for 1965 was being prepared, observations of a relevant nature were taken into account.

The question to ask yourself in such a matter is whether "since" and "while" in the nontime sense make your meaning clear. If so, you will be unwise to worry over such use of these words. What we need to be concerned about are not pinheads but major breaks in clarity. Critics who concern themselves with minutiae are often doing so instead of concentrating on basic content and clarity.

The old rule against the split infinitive was probably based on its awkwardness. Yet infinitives have been split with impunity—probably without notice—by Henry James and Mark Twain, to name only two writers. It is no secret that some infinitives are given their true sense only when split by the modifier.

> To make a profit, the price must be such that it returns to the company enough money to more than pay for all costs involved.

Some critics take refuge in rigid rules handed down from past generations. Language moves with the course of human events and words take on new guises. Old strictures concerning minor details of syntax are far less helpful in getting your message across than the underlying questions that you have to ask yourself: "Am I making myself clear? Am I being concise? Am I watching accuracy?" You need to become your own critic.

Often, the best revising is done by the drafter himself. He can see his own weaknesses by becoming aware of them. Finally, the drafter must double-check his statements. Secretaries may furnish inestimable aid, but one thing they do not do is to take the blame for mistakes on a page once it goes out.

The moral is clear. Scrutinize everything that leaves your desk. You are responsible, so proofread. If one decimal point can break a bank, it is worth checking. In the very strictness and exactness of the business situation lies not only your greatest obligation but your biggest boon.

Hersey's Report on Hiroshima

A difficult assignment was faced by author John Hersey in reporting on history's first atomic bombardment. His underlying problems in writing *Hiroshima* must have been solved in some systematic manner such as the one we have been discussing. The initial idea of his "report" originated either in his own mind or in the minds of *The New Yorker* editors, whose help he mentions in a prefatory note. His subject was as vast, as simple, and as awesome as the devastation of that Japanese city, and his purpose was to convey to readers in general the physical effect of the nuclear explosion, not necessarily to enlist people pro or con, not to advocate, or propose, or recommend. That the final impact of his report is, for most readers, an inescapable one is less a tribute to any argumentation than to his straight, factual presentation.

Upon finding workable limits for his subject hung all hope of success in fulfilling that purpose. This was managed by choosing six individuals as focal points and by marking off his coverage to one year precisely—August 6, 1945, to August 6, 1946.

To gather the abundance of factual data on which he drew, indeed to decide upon his plan of presentation, he went to Japan and talked with the survivors and walked among the city's ruins. Rather than allowing himself to be overwhelmed by all he saw and heard, he practiced "the selective art." Whatever Hersey's own reasons were for selecting the six individuals, the reader is left free to read into their experiences as much or as little of a representative nature as he wishes. Was it coincidence or part of Hersey's design that two of the six were women, deeply involved by their life-giving role; that two were doctors, professionally concerned with the work of life-preserving; and that two were members of the clergy, committed in their way to salvation itself. All were persons of primary responsibility for the human race.

When it came to organizing his material, all Hersey's skill and artistry came into play. Consistently, unremittingly, he went through the circumstances of disaster with each man and each woman he chose, finding out what they did on the eve of the explosion, at the hour of awakening on the next morning, on the sight of the flash; establishing the initial movements after it, the first human contacts, the efforts at survival, rescue, salvage; then recording reactions to the atomic rain, to the beginning of the fire, to the rumors—"What was it?"—and, eventually, their realization of the unsuspected truth, the attempts at recovery, the agonizing resumption of life and work.

The unity in Hersey's development of the subject comes from his meticulous arrangement of the material. The format, unlike that of a business report, makes use of chapter breaks and suggestive subtitles—suggestive by their very contrast in structure and tone. The horror, the haphazardry, is indicated stylistically by violation of the expected rather than by fulfillment of it, even in the wording used to describe it. As for the language, its concreteness, its stark objectivity, its rapid alterations in sentence length, its understatement, its use of detail, and its lack of superlatives are well suited to stimulating the reader's own emotional response.

Hersey's report on *Hiroshima,* in its presentation of data, organization, choice of language, clarity, and consideration of readers' interests, is a masterpiece of factual reporting. Such writing demonstrates the principles of communicating a difficult subject with a complex origin to a mass audience for an unmistakable effect.

Business, which needs to observe many of the same principles, provides a more specific commission for most of its reports. You know precisely what your subject is to be, what your purpose in tackling it is, who will read it. This makes the organizing, the drafting, and the revising so much the simpler. No matter how simple, how limited, how specific, if a matter is worth a written word, the principles of success are there for you to use.

Successful transmission of functional messages is achieved through awareness of three omnipresent elements: situation, style, and organization. Situation here is used to mean the circumstances surrounding writer and reader. Who is writing? You? In what capacity, then, are you writing? As a superior, subordinate, or equal? As a manager, a salesman, an engineer, a labor arbitrator?

To whom are you writing? On a clear visual image of your intended reader or on a careful estimate of any unknown readers hangs your hope of getting through. What does your reader need to know? What is he willing to hear in the given circumstances?

What are you writing about and, equally important, why are you writing? How are you transmitting your message? Perhaps you should not be writing at all; there is always the telephone and often the chance for a face-to-face meeting. And when and where is your communication going? To the office down the hall? To the president of your company or to the manager responsible to you? Will the message arrive early, late, or at the moment of the reader's need for it? These are the questions that enable you to size up your situation.

Having thrashed out the answers in terms of the circumstances, you resort to words, sentences, and paragraphs. This is what we mean by style. Your style is uniquely yours, for better or for worse. No two people word their messages in precisely the same way. Style is developed individually from the common pool of language but out of the special experiences of the writer.

Organization, in regard to communicating, refers to matters of sequence. How do you get started? What do you say first, next, and next, and next? And, of equal perplexity: how do you close? Where do you want to leave your reader?

Sequence and wording are those parts of a document which are visible on the piece of paper. Invisible, like the part of an iceberg below the water's surface, is the situation giving rise to the organization and the style.

2: Relating Words to Objectives

In spite of the outcries of business against poor writing, the specific qualities desired are seldom specified. Fred C. Foy, of the Koppers Company, believes in principle that "no matter how good a man's ideas are, if he can't communicate them effectively they won't be much good either to him or to the business for which he works." Raymond Kendall, Itek Laboratories, argues: "Effective communication involves conscious study and practice." But what is meant by communicating "effectively?"

Do business leaders want more or less grammar? sharper expression with no face-saving ambiguity? a more or a less casual tone? a persuasive or an objective approach? more or less directness?

When it comes right down to answering these questions, you as the writer have to know what you wish, in the circumstances, to convey. Does business as a whole have any common language policy? One who has come close to a tangible proposal is Theodore O. Yntema, Vice-President of the Ford Motor Company: "The first requisite to effective communication is clarity and organization of your own thoughts. The second is understanding of your audience. The third is just plain hard work to achieve a good job." Here we have a workmanlike statement about how to write.

A Language Policy

Ways of writing business communications need to vary as in other creative forms—dramas, novels, professional articles, TV scripts, case histories, newspaper stories. Not only does each situation vary, but so does each person. The businessman is an individual first and a businessman second; his style of writing will be as much a reflection of his personality as are his face, his voice, and his walk.

People who are actually engaged in the paper work of business, when asked to identify their objectives in developing writing skill, answer variously:

> I must let them know exactly what response I am after. At the same time, I have to use as favorable a tone in my writing as I can.

> I am an officer manager at a hospital. I supervise 31 women. The two primary functions of my office are to keep an accurate accounting record of patients and collect all monies due from them. . . . I want to write my ideas for training employees with color and impact. The material written must sell an idea. It is not sufficient to state the factual processes of doing a job to get a job well done.

> Concentrating on the functions of the Controller's activity, I find that the three ideal qualities of written communication for my job are:
> 1. The ability to know my reader and to write for him.
> 2. The foresight to make a compromise between speed and completeness.
> 3. The objectivity to write for a positive goal rather than away from the negative.

> I will talk about banking, and I will talk about business reports. . . . the format, the physical appearance, should be designed for easy reading. Bankers are busy people. They will probably not take the time to read reports that have the appearance of being "tough to read." . . . the report writer in banking should be conservative in his style or tone. This involves strict adherence to grammatical rules and spelling rules.

> I find, now, that my most effective letters are written when I sit down and actually carry on a conversation

> with the reader in my mind. This helps me to put myself in his place and increase the "you-attitude" without forsaking clarity.

On this much, twentieth-century business agrees. We are reacting against nineteenth-century superformalism, its upward-downward intonation, its indirectness, its grammatical and rhetorical preciosity. Clarity, conciseness, accuracy, adaptation, directness, and positiveness lead among the current goals. The days of the carriage trade are over, and so is its idiom. Language is a weather vane of its era. To prescribe one policy for good writing is to risk missing the particular writer's particular mark. Knowledge of the possibilities, the variations, and the controlling factors in policy is what we need.

More basic than mere repetition of the need for better writing, more pertinent than agreement upon goals, is a working knowledge of the three ingredients of ordinary writing: the word, the sentence, the paragraph. These are the "clay and wattles" of language.

The Word

"We know that many tools are available to us in the mechanics of communication," wrote a spokesman for Kenyon Eckhardt, Inc., the firm which won a recent award from the Advertising Writers Club of New York. Kenyon Eckhardt believes that the most important "of the many tools in advertising is first: 'The Word.' " And the poster which won the award shows the silhouetted figure of Sir Winston Churchill with a caption beginning: "He could have said, 'We owe a lot to the R.A.F. . . .' " Instead, of course, he chose the words: "Never . . . was so much owed by so many to so few."

In choosing your words for the purposes of everyday, what are some of the obvious alternatives?

Concrete or Abstract

No longer does the professional person jeopardize his reputation by using the simple, specific word instead of a sixty-four-dollar counterpart. In selecting your words, recognize the impact of the concrete versus the abstract. Hersey can be sampled at random to illustrate this quality. With Hiroshima burning, Tanimoto "went to the river again, the basin in his hand, and jumped down onto a sandpit." You can see each object, each action. The author is talking in name words, picture words. He leaves no doubt as to what he is reporting.

The difference in the effect when you use concrete words as contrasted with abstract ones speaks for itself. The effect of concrete words ("spade" versus "digging implement") is to create a clear, definite image in the reader's mind. Why not call a spade just that? The effect of abstract wording—sometimes preferred, it should be acknowledged—is apt to be one of conceptual, all-inclusive possibilities. Here is what one management consultant wrote his client company in the course of an engagement:

> We recommend, therefore, that a further evaluation be made of present policies, methods, and procedures applicable to historical operating standards. As a result of this evaluation, a program would be developed for more effective use of them in accomplishing the objectives.

The consultant probably did not wish to tell his client in concrete words that the XYZ Company should see what, if any, changes had taken place in its way of doing business. Is the company now producing and selling more—and at what rate of profit—this year as compared, say, with ten years ago? If the answer is No, the company has not improved, changes should be made. Though writing in abstractions slows up the reader's intake, there are times when the rapid, inescapable, explicit sense is not what the writer wants.

On the other hand, a reader gets impatient with evasion by means of vocabulary. The dilemma of one graduate student over his thesis subject evoked obvious sympathy from the newspaper which told his story:

> The title of his thesis was: "Why the Foreman Hates

> the Boss." The thesis was accepted, but the title was changed to something like "Emotional Coefficient Correlatives in Interpersonal Relationships between Management and Supervisory Echelons."

"Hate" is easier to visualize than an "emotional coefficient correlative," and so on. The effect between the two ways of saying what the author had in mind is entirely different. It is only necessary to determine what effect is desired.

Short or Long

Sometimes a situation rules out a sharp, clear-cut statement. The writer then retreats behind the abstract, polysyllabic terminology which is open to several meanings. One United States governmental department answered a request for an official definition of the term "preference customer" this way:

> The broad question of preference customer qualification is one which is not well suited to discussion in generalities and on the basis of hypothetical considerations. Unfortunately, when discussing such a subject in general and hypothetical terms, either question or response is apt to give a misleading impression because one or another theoretical or hypothetical factor may be singled out for emphasis and the subject is then prone to be viewed against a set of limited conditions and qualifications which may have little relationship to actual facts and circumstances as they develop and in the light of which the particular status in fact of a given customer will ultimately have to be determined.

There is scarcely a tangible word in the lot: nothing to get your hands on. Feeling more confused than before, the inquirer phoned Washington, D. C. The difficulty, it turned out, lay in the sensitive nature of the subject. Here is what the inquirer wrote down as he held the receiver:

> A preference customer generally is a customer that is given preference in the sale of Federal power and generally means public bodies and cooperatives. For

> more information . . . refer to the Federal Power Acts, namely, the Flood Control Act of 1944.

Long, wide-open words do serve the purpose of ambiguity if that is the writer's intent and need. The need is father to the word.

"Ambiguity and vagueness," averred a public relations man for one huge industrial concern, "in correspondence, in speeches, in many printed communications in business, especially among industrial mammoths, frequently are deliberate, designed, planned. . . . Writing of top management in business," continued this seasoned practitioner, "has been forced in this century to adopt the techniques used effectively by those in the arena of international diplomacy. The trick is to sound clear, brief, sincere, and purposive but to remain vague."

Ambiguity, necessary as it occasionally seems, is not primarily what makes business—or action of any sort—productive. To speed up action, the writer must make each word unmistakable. Consider again Churchill's thirty-three words:

> . . . we shall fight on the beaches, we shall fight on the landing grounds, we shall fight in the fields and on the streets, we shall fight in the hills; we shall never surrender.

Perhaps it was by intent that these are chiefly one-syllable name words, used with the first-person pronoun. It was the great Fowler of the *Dictionary of Modern English Usage* who pointed out that, in English, it is the native words which are short and the foreign words which are long. "Home" is an Anglo-Saxon word, as are "chew" and "day," for example.

Right or Wrong

The purposes of business are usually served by words that are concrete and short and properly spelled. Spelling may not be a rational matter, but everyone got the point in the humorous book by Edward Streeter, *Dere Mable,* the love letters of a World War I rookie. The rookie was a good-natured simpleton whose misspelling was his earmark. Proper spelling may be no more than a matter of prejudice. Though other linguistic prejudices are giving way, correct spelling remains a basic requirement on most jobs, whether it devolves upon the secretary or not. Only the foolhardy individual operates without a desk dictionary. It is not that you are expected to be a born speller; you are expected merely to pay your reader the courtesy of looking things up.

The particular words most subject to misuse vary according to fields of work. A few samples cut across most fields. "Affect" and "effect" are common confusers, unless distinguished as in this composite passage:

Effect as a noun	In a business letter, the use of white space produces an eye-saving effect. A good margin is, in effect, essential to you. Like your pen and stationery, your notebook of letters can be amongst your most valuable effects.
Effect as a verb (always transitive)	To effect a change for the better, leave ample margins on your page.
Affect as a verb (now generally transitive)	Some writers affect a casual, informal appearance in a letter by a crowded, irregularly-spaced page. A crowded page will usually affect the letter's readability adversely.

Another source of error is traceable to the ear: "Poe writes perceptibly," comments one literary enthusiast whose eye and ear played tricks with the adverb "perceptively." The reason why "type" as a noun is moving over to the position of an adjective is also an auditory reason: "This type of day," "This type of drug," "This type of ship," are expressions which, when repeated over and over by broadcasters, begin to sound like: "This type day," This type drug," "This type ship." So the "of" actually disappears from the written version, and "type" no longer sets apart a special class or group of events, drugs, or ships, but instead loosely describes in adjectival fashion a similarity. In the course of such deterioration of meaning, the next stage is clear. "Type" will move out of its position as an adjective to that of a mere prefix: "This typeday," This typedrug," "This typeship." "I could of gone" is another corruption attributable to sound ("I could have gone"). Mrs. Malaprop, the incomparable creation of the playwright Richard Brinsley Sheridan, still heads the list of those who use words by sound rather than by sense, words that are malapropos or malapropisms:

> "I would by no means wish a daughter of mine," declared she, "to be a *progeny* of learning. . . . She should have a *supercilious* knowledge in accounts. . . . I would have her instructed in *geometry,* that she might know something of the *contagious* countries. But above all . . . she should be mistress of *orthodoxy* that she might not mis-spell and mis-pronounce words. . . . and likewise that she might *reprehend* the true meaning of what she is saying."

People's levels of correctness vary. Many object violently to "finalize" despite the fact that Dwight D. Eisenhower as President made frequent use of it. "Facilitization," which is thoroughly familiar and acceptable in one automotive concern, still seems barbarous to some. Newness in itself is not the reason why a word is objectionable. Terms may be created unnecessarily or built up out of a benighted sense of emphasis by piling up suffixes or prefixes on the good old simple name for the same thing. "Irregardless" is a glaring illustration of this process. "Enumerous" comes from the same syndrome.

Few or Many

To be told you are a man of few words is to be given high praise in business life. Using more words than are necessary in making your point is asking for more time than your reader is going to give you. Some writers develop the habit of doing a double-take: an "important and interesting" experiment, a "clear and simple" process, a "fair and equitable" share, a "valuable and worthwhile" experience. Say a thing once by finding the precise word. You can argue that there is a difference between "important" and "interesting," between "clear" and "simple," between "fair" and "equitable," between "valuable" and "worth-while," but splitting hairs is not usually your point.

Wording is built up endlessly on the false idea that the more words there are, the more emphatic the impression. Quite the contrary. Beyond a point, repetition defeats itself. Most readers are canny, quick to resist going over the same ground. Even though the document may be perused to its remote finale, the reader may long before the end cease to take it in, being resentful of the extra verbiage. Just as people with hearing aids can switch them off if there is too much noise, so readers can become blind to long, drawn-out writing. Cutting is usually the easiest way for a writer to improve his effect.

Omnipresent words such as "tend to" and "based on" can often be dropped without being missed. Their presence may serve only to block off meaning. One of these offenders, "based," is often placed in a freestanding position so that it is itself not "based" on anything. What, in the following example, does "based" relate to or modify? "Based on the data the office manager will compute the commissions." Surely the office manager is not based on the data.

The use of such escape hatches as "and/or," "etc.," "et al." are usually for escape only. They compel the reader to do the work of figuring out the meaning, a responsibility that belongs to the writer. What does the author really have in mind when he says: "Pressure on accounting to know how costs will behave under varying conditions, suppositions, etc., has become more pronounced"? Such extra expressions as "it is true that" and "serve to" are worth their salt only if needed for emphasis.

Even Mark Twain accused himself of using more words than necessary:

> My dear Howells:
>
> Herewith is the proof. In spite of myself, how awkwardly I do jumble words together and how often I

> do use three words where one would answer—a thing I am always trying to guard against. I shall become as slovenly a writer as Charles Francis Adams if I don't look out. (That is said in jest, because of course I do not seriously fear getting so bad as that.) I never shall drop so far toward his and Bret Harte's level as to catch myself saying, "It must have been wiser to have believed that he might have accomplished it if he could have felt that he would have been supported by those who should have etc. etc. etc." . . .
>
> Yrs ever
> Mark

Apt or Trite

Words get shopworn. These are the trite ones which, when written as they so often are in tandem, lead us into over-familiar, stereotyped phraseology: "At your convenience," "don't hesitate," "enclosed is," "prompt attention," or "feel free." George Orwell, in his essay "Politics and the English Language," shows how staleness leads to meaninglessness or worse. He would have enjoyed the cartoon in *Dublin Opinion* showing a pompous gentleman dictating to his bored secretary:

> Er—I am directed by the Minister to state that he has —er—given sympathetic consideration to your application but that, in the present situation, etc., etc., . . . and then go on and tell him, in the usual formula, that he hasn't a hope in hell.

Of course, some word formulas, like the salutations and complimentary closes of letters, have a perfunctory purpose. And there are spoken words like "hello" and "good-by" without which we would be lost. International currency has been gained for the expression "o.k." In a cut and dried context, some cut and dried expressions are indispensable. It is understandable why *pro forma* expressions occur very often at the beginning and end of a communication. These are the spots where the communicator wishes to show courtesy, cordiality, or simple friendliness to his reader, and this is often hard to do. Such a goal is best attained by the individualized, pertinent phraseology of the communication and by the relationship of the writer and reader.

The harder the situation surrounding a written communication, the more likely the writer is to bring forth words and phrases circling around in his memory instead of phrasing his own words for the occasion. The young man preparing his first job application, for instance, feels insecure about what to expect, hopeful but fearful. So he falls ready victim to certain pat jargonology. An actual census of application letters from some five hundred students of business administration showed repeated use of these particular expressions:

. . . become acquainted with
. . . could be an asset
. . . would welcome the opportunity
. . . have been exposed to
. . . share my growth with you
. . . learn through doing
. . . plan to make my career in
. . . to further my career goals
. . . have become familiar with
. . . happy to answer any questions
. . . with an eye toward
. . . to know each other better
. . . with an aptitude for
. . . not just a route to
. . . has come to my attention
. . . handling groups of people
. . . has taught me people's reactions
. . . how people act
. . . my experience with people
. . . ability to get along with people
. . . how to work with people
. . . the ability to make friends
. . . to communicate with people
. . . a diversified background
. . . a background in
. . . well-rounded background
. . . tool courses

. . . has given me an insight
. . . has given me valuable experience

Not only is such patois of the application situation tiresomely familiar to personnel directors, but it betrays the writers' lack of individuality, and, what's worse, an unintended pretentiousness. The young applicant who avers his "insight into people" and his "diversified background" is only saying what he thinks he should say under the circumstances, not giving specific information related to himself and his prospective employment.

A ready-made set of words, pulled down off the shelf of memory, will scarcely register in the reader's mind: "Please feel free to write again," Don't hesitate to let me know," "Thank you in advance for your consideration." (The latter is not only trite, but it tempts a sarcastic rebuttal.) The reader has seen such expressions too many times before.

Difficult letters may, of course, have to end on a perfunctory note but what makes the reader react best is a conclusion drafted specifically for him, such as: "May I have your comments soon?" William Faulkner, whose love of the language led him into its farthest corners, put this wry observation into the mouth of one of his characters, the young boy of *Intruder in the Dust*:

> . . . he heard for the third time almost exactly what he had heard twice in twelve hours, and he marvelled again at the paucity, the really almost standardized meagreness not of individual vocabularies but of Vocabulary itself. . . .

When you are actually talking turkey, call the turkey a turkey. Find a fresh, fitting expression, not that which is honored by time and time alone. A longer word, applied for the first time to a particular situation, adds a new dimension and may be the best one for the moment. Those sayings that are prefabricated lack the appeal of pertinence.

Direct or Mechanical

Then there are expressions which are purely mechanical. "This report is about the question of company investment in the drug industry" is a mechanical way to begin. In writing, mechanics do not get to the heart of the matter.

After your first draft, after the walls are up, why not tear down the scaffolding from which you built? Begin simply, "Our company is considering investment in the drug industry." Often as not, you can blue-pencil words like: "This memo is . . .," "You asked for . . .," "The purpose of this paper. . . ." E. B. White in *The Elements of Style* tells us how his old grammar teacher, William Strunk, reviled the phrase, "the fact that. . . ."

You as the drafter may at first need to spell out your own thoughts laboriously in a mechanical way; you may have to put down on paper "the fact that" something follows from something else. If that something does actually follow, if your report is actually about what you say it is about, the reader should usually be able to see as much for himself.

Of course, there will be passages in which you are dealing with such complex material that you may have to reveal the machinery that makes the wheels turn. "See above" is employed with the best of intentions, even when "above" is not above but a half-dozen pages back. More often than not, the material should speak for itself, as in this reference to ultrahigh-voltage lines from an annual report of the American Electric Power Company, Inc.:

> These lines will: provide lower transmission cost per kilowatt delivered; through interconnections, facilitate the pooling of power and make possible reduced reserve capacity needs; and minimize requirements for line rights-of-way—all resulting in very substantial savings in construction and operation.

The author could have said: "These lines will do the following: . . ." Fortunately, he realized there was no need to beat the reader over the head. Readers can be insulted by being told, unnecessarily, where to look for what.

Other crutch words like "accordingly," "however," "therefore," and "thus" abound in business communications. Sometimes essential, they are also used to prop up limping logic or to coerce the reader's understanding. The legal profession could not safely be divested of its favorite "aforementioned." Not so in the business profession, which has its own objectives, its own situational controls. To increase the interest of a reader, avoid mechanical words. If, instead of dragging a horse to water, you lead him gently but firmly, you don't have to make him drink. Give your reader the pleasure of discovering relationships for himself rather than drag him along with compulsive wording.

Objective or Subjective

It is easy to see the value of short, correct, nonmechanistic, name words, sparingly used, but it is a little harder to distinguish between words called objective (or "descriptive") and words called subjective (or "emotive"). Do you want to report that a committee "arrived at" a decision or that it "hammered" it out? There is a distinct difference. It is easy to see that you do something different according to which kind of word you use, and you need to take the difference into consideration ahead of time. "Arrived at" is the objective wording; "hammered out" is the subjective.

Business is attracted by the conveying power, the magic, of words. "Open Sesame" was uttered and a mountain yawned. "Abracadabra" and "hocus-pocus" are like the wave of the hypnotist's hands. Among the beliefs Londoners held about warding off the plague, according to Daniel Defoe in his *Journal of the Plague Year,* was this: ". . . it [the plague] was to be kept off with crossings, signs of the zodiac, . . . and certain words . . . as particularly the word Abracadabra. . . ." Any objective, descriptive sense such expressions may have had has long since succumbed to the subjective, emotive sense. Abracadabra has no meaning apart from legerdemain. Advertising has capitalized upon its ability to identify words, apart from and often in contradiction to dictionary definitions, with emotional connotations akin to magic. A *New Yorker* cartoon by Kraus on this propensity showed a harried ad man: "Our problem," he told his co-workers, "is to get across to the American public that fattening foods are non-fattening." The word becomes the master over the thing itself, as Humpty Dumpty once implied, when we choose the "jumbo" or "giant" quart as compared to the ordinary quart. A quart is a quart.

If you're going to be master of your words, as Humpty Dumpty said to Alice in *Through the Looking Glass,* decide whether you want to convey fact? feeling? one or both? Go back to your purpose: is it to inform? to persuade? to do one or both?

In another kind of attempt to use words for their mastery or magic, the New York Transit Authority posted in its subways cartoons headed "Three Magic Words." The cartoons showed scenes such as a young mother taking her child on her lap to make room for an old gentleman. He says "Please." She says "Sorry" as she makes way for him. He replies "Thanks." Everyone is happy. Less magic was generated by mere terminology in a recent dispute between employers and employees at *The Detroit News.* The strikers termed the company's action a "lock out." Management termed it a "strike." But the mere wording did not convince the other side or produce the magic of a settlement.

In another labor dispute, this one between the Civil Service Commission of Nassau County, New York, and a group of its employees at the Meadowbrook Hospital, nomenclature was, on the surface at least, the issue. The employees, previously classed specifically by trades as painters, plumbers, carpenters, and electricians, were reclassified by the commission in one group as maintenance men. The employees protested eloquently against being lumped together as "an undistinguishable unit in a mass society": "Today, much of a man's status in his community depends on the title of his job," wrote their representative. The commission, unmoved by the plea, cited the dictionary's definition of "maintenance" in adhering to the reclassification. It is a fair question whether economic factors were also at stake in this controversial reclassification. Semantics served both parties as the overt reason. A name may fulfill diverse purposes. In the course of the controversy, each side chose to stand on the issue of wording; if matters of wages and working conditions were involved, they were never put in writing. When semantics are a front, recourse to the dictionary may be a front also. Aside from labor relations, other aspects of business such as marketing become involved with the significance of a mere word.

When the Ford Motor Company produced a compact car, the naming of it was not treated as a light matter. "Changing a name," said Ford's marketing research manager, "creates more emotional disturbance in a company than anything we do." Surveys were made; of the 10,000 possible names, nine were singled out for consideration on the basis of symbolic content, and then two: Falcon and Futura. The decision went to Falcon for several reasons, according to the research manager: ". . . The Falcon is the strongest bird in the world. It is the most agile bird. It is graceful. It is very dramatic in motion. Finally, it soars to great heights."

Words have powers beyond their objective, descriptive definitions. They induce action, and the action may resemble an involuntary reflex. The dictionary tells you only part of the story. The sacredness of certain name words to Londoners became apparent recently. The names included those of five authors, four admirals, three historians, two musicians, and a painter. They are also the names of some of London's telephone exchanges. The telephone company wanted to convert to direct dialing for long distance. All-number codes have, in the course of conversion elsewhere, replaced exchange names. British officials, however, declined to approve giving up the familiar names. Their reasoning, whatever their sentiment, is objective; to wit, that it is easier to remember telephone numbers of three or four digits plus "Wordsworth" or "Trevelyan" than it is to remember six- and seven-digit numbers. The appeal of such familiar and prideful names as those of the London Telephone Company may help people to remember.

Any writer needs to be aware of all he is actually imparting by his words. Justice Oliver Wendell Holmes went further than most persons, but he had a point when he wrote: "I rarely look at a dictionary, which after all is merely somebody's estimate of polite usage, a matter on which one can form one's own opinion." Titles in government, in education, in business are constantly being upgraded. People become deputies instead of assistants, directors general instead of directors. To give status is one semantic possibility. To give a noninvidious impression is another, which explains why "underdeveloped" or "emerging" countries have become "developing" countries. "Nonproductive" labor has become, in some plants, "indirect" labor as distinct from "productive" or "direct." Though "nondestructive" engineers have not yet objected to that terminology as it is applied to them, how long before they will?

Words are usually chosen for their meaning, whether objective or subjective. Seldom is it necessary to find a name that is as meaningless as possible. Yet that seems to have been the problem confronting the United States Atomic Energy Commission when nuclear testing was resumed in 1962 in the Pacific. The test series was named "Operation Dominic." As noted in the announcement made at the time, this is a masculine proper name with a Latin ancestry, and it was not chosen for any particular significance. It was simply taken from a list of available code names maintained by the Defense Department. The controversy at home and abroad surrounding the resumption of testing necessitated avoidance of any ideologically loaded word.

General or Special

Far from magical is the specialized word, the technical vocabulary of the expert, or to call it by the "emotive" word for it—jargon. Is jargon justifiable? To say the answer "all depends," though scarcely an answer, is true. Jargon has become a target of attack because of its epidemic proportions.

Each new specialty in this specializing age soon builds its own jargon or private vocabulary. In this, business is only doing what special groups in society have always done. "Cool" talk of "dig me," "daddy-o," "far out" came with the beatniks. Gang terms like to "jap," and to "punk out" came from the sidewalks of New York. A "MAD" (Michigan Algorithm Decoder) language has appeared among engineers for programming certain computers. The secret codes or ciphers used by international intelligence agents represent the tightest kind of control on intelligibility, of course.

Business with its mounting specialization has given new meaning to old words: "All blankets which have been forecasted to exceed $100,000 should be submitted annually," wrote a finance man, who used "blanket," he explained, to mean "any undertaking to achieve a specific objective." The purpose is partly to save time. The purpose also, in coining a particularized meaning, is to prevent ambiguity. An automobile safety engineer wrote: "A small amount of oxygen is consumed for hand and machine scarfing in the Rolling Mill, culling the Skull Cracker, torch work in the Stripper Building, and iron cutting in the Blast Furnaces." Athletes have a terminology all their own, game by game. Medical, legal, and scientific parlances are each *sui generis.*

No sooner had the United States sent aloft its first astronaut than a whole new glossary appeared: "T-time" for take-off, "chicken switch" for escape device, "go" and "no go" for last-moment signal, "cherry picker" for rescue lift, "A-OK" for everything all right. The lack, however, of a sufficiently particularized word caused trouble for the first man to orbit the earth. Lieutenant Colonel John H. Glenn referred to a "blackout" in connection with his re-entry. Some listeners jumped to the conclusion that he meant a loss of consciousness. What he really meant was that atmospheric conditions would put him out of communication with his ground team temporarily. In explaining this confusion over a commonly used term, Colonel Glenn later suggested that astronauts might need a new word: "comloss." To be exact in the exact—even unique—situation, may necessitate creation of new and exact terminology. Ambiguity may be costly and dangerous.

Specialized wording has disadvantages. By cutting down the number of people who can understand, the audience is automatically restricted. Only the initiated will get the point. The more technical the term, the fewer who will comprehend. From this disadvantage arises another. A writer may parade his own supply of special terms, knowing that his reader will not understand. The hope, perhaps unrecognized, is to impress, to dazzle.

Such a hope has little place in business reports, or in other kinds of writing according to the late Ernest Hemingway. As a badge of exclusiveness, jargon fools few nowadays. In his account of bullfighting in "The Dangerous Summer," Hemingway specified:

> I am trying to avoid using a Spanish word whenever I can explain in idiomatic English. This is not always possible but I think it is better than the peppering, larding and truffleing with bullfight terms and phrases that you get from the newly erudite writers . . . You could be so snowed under with Manoletinas, Giraldillas, Pedresinas, Trincherillas and other varieties of ballroom bananas that you could not see the paper for the words.

The use of fancy terminology to make your reader slip is seldom the objective in business.

But technical wording has its uses. Where would a doctor or a scientist be without his own vocabulary? Those in the know are not heard objecting to the terminologies of their own professions. Used at the right time and place, the specialized expressions of business can transmit a fact or idea without verbosity or vagueness. Their usefulness depends on when and where they are employed. No one has criticized Jonathan Swift's very private jargon, the "baby talk" or "little language" in which he wrote to his beloved Stella. To all except her, the letters remain partially unintelligible and so he intended.

Loose and nontechnical use of ordinary words is another sort of jargon, harder to justify: "finalize," "type," "meaningful," "rewarding" are words in vogue for an altered sense, and they often carry an air of affectation rather than of specialized sense. "Area," for instance, is a word strewn throughout some reports like a handful of raisins thrown into cake batter. It means everything and nothing. "Tool" will soon meet the same fate.

Summing Up

To sum up word choice: use as few words as possible. Make them short, concrete, correct, fresh, direct. Distinguish between objective and subjective meanings. Remember who your reader is and what your purpose is in using specialized terms. Communication often is most needed between persons engaged in different specialties.

3: Managing Sentences and Paragraphs

As the basic unit of communication, the word offers you numerous choices if you are in search of accuracy, brevity, and clarity. The larger units of style into which you cast your chosen words are the sentence and the paragraph.

The Sentence

Length and Structure

As a unit of communication, the sentence offers endless variations and combinations. The plea has been made for the short, simple sentence in business affairs. The reason is that most writers can be sure in this way of correct construction and can therefore be clearer. It is relatively easy to use one subject with one predicate so that they make sense together. To write all your sentences this way is a mistake. Any repetitious pattern spells monotony; the sentences begin to stab the reader.

Not only will variety keep your reader going, but he can cover the ground faster if you use dependent as well as independent clauses, if you intersperse modifying phrases, if you inject a question now and then. Continuous employment of the simple subject-verb pattern is the work of the routineer. Interest comes from a shift in pattern and a shift in length.

In a short sentence, it is hard to build a climax. Not only that, but it is hard in a short sentence to develop a series, itself a way of saying a good deal quickly. In spite of such points, shortness in a sentence is particularly valuable in business affairs. The mind takes in one idea at a time and then sees the connections.

Churchill, in the course of his long career, demonstrated

his flexibility. As a wartime leader, he became the master of terse structure. His purpose was often achieved by short, simple, declarative sentences in succession, but he never confined himself to any one pattern. Peacetime produced in him a different style. In looking back upon his wartime leadership, he used a sentence of seventy-five words to sum it all up:

> Thus, then, on the night of the tenth of May, at the outset of this mighty battle, I acquired the chief power in the State, which henceforth I wielded in ever-growing measure for five years and three months of world war, at the end of which time, all our enemies having surrendered unconditionally or being about to do so, I was immediately dismissed by the British electorate from all further conduct of their affairs.

The climax is telling.

Long sentences are harder to write well. Like long skirts, they may trip up the wearer, but only if not properly handled. One sentence of two hundred and twelve words in an edition of the Government's instructions, *How to Prepare Your Income Tax Return on Form 1041,* so infuriated a senator that he offered a prize to the person who could say the same thing briefly, clearly, and still accurately.

One of the risks you take in lengthening your sentences is misplacing modifying words. Modifiers need to stand close to the word or words being modified; otherwise the reader will not know where they belong so far as sense is concerned:

> The report is forwarded to the Central Staff attached to a cover letter . . . (Is the Central Staff attached to a cover letter?)

> This calf ratio means that on the average it required 1.3 mature breeding animals to produce one calf. (Was it the requirement for which an average was being given? No, it was the number of breeding animals.)

Within a sentence, be sure related words are properly juxtaposed.

A particular kind of misplaced modifier is the dangling participle. The participial form of the verb, whether it ends in "–ed" or "–ing," may be used to modify other words. Many sentences have such words at or near the beginning, as does this explanation of a gate-control form at an automotive plant:

> After entering the time and date, verifying the status of the load, determining the allowability of time lapses, and presenting a completed copy to the driver, the truck is released.

Because "entering," "verifying," "determining," and "presenting" describe what someone or something did, the question is what? The sentence says "the truck." The real doer is missing: the gatekeeper, of course. So we have a dangling modifier, as in many instances of unrelatedness:

> Assuming that the $15,000 per year was received for the 10-year lease, a $150,000 total amount cannot be considered to have a present value of more than $110,400.

Who is doing the "assuming"? Dangling modifiers have absentee ownership. There are specialists on the language who do not classify dangling participles as incorrect so long as the reader can get the meaning. A functional style which aims at delivery of unmistakable meaning in as short time as possible cannot be left to guesswork on the reader's part. Incomplete or ambiguous structure amounts to just that.

Misplacement of the word "both" either in a long or short sentence can cause ambiguity: "Paper work in both branches and home office should be studied" must be corrected to: "Paper work both in the branches and the home office . . ." Another word that often falsifies the sense because of standing away from what it really modifies is "only."

The chief danger from length is overloading the sentence. Overloading comes from trying to say too much between a capital letter and a period. As you can see for yourself, it slows down and befuddles the reader:

> Our review and lists of the statistical data employed in the computations of the liability showed that the listings of services paid by month and year incurred were not reconciled by the Association to the total paid for the month as shown by the Account Book summary.

The original author had no trouble in revising as soon as he saw the need to do so.

The more a person advances professionally, the more at home he becomes in his special subject matter, the more he inclines to write long sentences. He, as the writer, no longer has any trouble seeing the interrelationships of his facts and ideas. Intent upon conveying these qualifying connections to his reader, he combines them in one sentence. Overloading of that frail vehicle results. Younger men, new on a job and still feeling their own way, are often the ones whose sentences are short and gradual in content. Their thoughts still come that way. So what is needed in keeping the tracks clear is continual concentration on the destination: clear comprehension by the reader.

Incomplete sentences, once a sure path to ignominy, are appearing in functional writing more and more:

> The condition persisted. Each month the customer paid the charge for the current period, and each month the payment was applied to the arrears. The result, a constant unpaid balance.

Sentence fragments, if used by intent and if used inoffensively like the one at the end of the quoted passage, may suggest a thought which the reader has the satisfaction of completing for himself. Like participation in sports, reader participation is one way to hold interest. But it is taking liberties with language, and to take liberties you need to be sure of your ground. A householder, in a letter protesting a bill, appears to have been unaware of using an incomplete sentence:

> Your gas company failed to convey two things. First, that you have an automatic bill of $1.90 each month. This amount is charged even if no gas is used. Secondly, that a bill is sent to each customer every month.

As a demonstration of the different results obtainable from different sentence and word patterns, here are two examples of approximately one hundred words each, both by widely known authors. (The styles are obviously distinct, one from another.) Which one do you comprehend more quickly and easily? Why?

> (First author)
> When I was a boy there was but one permanent ambition among my comrades in our village on the west bank of the Mississippi River. That was to be a steamboatman. We had transient ambitions of other sorts but they were only transient. When a circus came and went, it left us all burning to become clowns; the first Negro minstrel show that ever came to our section left us all suffering to try that kind of life; now and then we had a hope that, if we lived and were good, God would permit us to be pirates. These ambitions faded out, each in its turn; but the ambition to be a steamboatman always remained.

> (Second author)
> He so felt the blow indeed, so gasped, before what had happened to him, at the ugliness, the bitterness, and, beyond these things, the sinister strangeness, that, the matter of his dismay little by little detaching and projecting itself, settling there face to face with him as something he must now live with always, he might have been in charge of some horrid alien thing, some violent, scared, unhappy creature whom there was small joy, of a truth, in remaining with, but whose behaviour wouldn't perhaps bring him under notice, nor otherwise compromise him, so long as he should stay to watch it.

The first passage consists of five sentences: the first, a complex one; the second, simple; the third, compound; the fourth, complex; the fifth, compound. Independent and dependent clauses are intermingled, there being nine of the former and five of the latter. For the total 116 words, there are 155 syllables. There are over a score of verbs, fourteen pronouns, mostly personal, and twenty-four nouns, of which half are concrete (like "boy," "comrades," "village," "steamboatman," "clowns," "pirates"). In no more than a couple of words ("burning," "faded") is the language figurative; the paragraph is literal in meaning. Taken from *Old Times on the Mississippi,* the writing is Mark Twain's.

The second passage consists of one complex sentence made up of six dependent clauses attached to one independent clause. For the total 103 words, there are 145 syllables. There are fourteen verbs, fourteen pronouns, mostly personal, and seventeen nouns, of which all but three are abstract and figurative as well. In fact, the entire paragraph is built on a figure of speech. Taken from "A Round of Visits," the writing is Henry James's.

You probably found the results of reading the paragraphs were not the same. The quick, easy impact of the one contrasts with the vague, suggestive effect of the other. What is there in the styles of writing that may account for the difference in impressions conveyed to the reader? First, we

WORDING DIFFERENCES IN PASSAGES OF TWO AUTHORS

Number of:	Mark Twain	Henry James
Syllables	155	145
Words	116	103
Clauses:	14	7
Independent	9	1
Dependent	5	6
Sentences:	5	1
Simple	1	0
Compound	2	0
Complex	2	1
Verbs	20	14
Nouns	24	17
Pronouns	14	14
Figurative/Abstract Words	2	11

need to rule out any similarities: the frequency of personal pronouns is almost the same. The average length of words —that is, the number of syllables per word—is not significantly dissimilar. What, now, about the length of sentence? Mark Twain averages 20 words, Henry James, 103. What about the number of independent and dependent clauses? Mark Twain has almost two for one; Henry James, one for six. Mark Twain has a higher proportion of action words (verbs) and name words (nouns). The most conspicuous differentiation in the two styles, however, occurs in the nature of the nouns: in the first selection the majority are concrete terms naming a tangible person ("boy"), place ("river"), or thing ("circus") and are meant to be taken literally. In the second selection the nouns with a few exceptions are either abstract concepts (like "ugliness," "strangeness," "dismay," "behaviour") and therefore intangible, or else they are figurative (like "blow," "face," "creature") and thereby necessitate a process of interpretation on the part of the reader.

Having used for the experiment two established and esteemed authors, we cannot possibly say one is good and one is bad. It may be possible for you to say one is faster to read than the other, or easier to comprehend, or more memorable. Any preference you may now be feeling needs to be related to the probable intent of the author, just as your own style should, in all fairness, be judged in the light of what you want to accomplish.

This much is obvious. From the point of view of the reader, short, complete sentences are apt to be read quickly without the reader's misconstruing them. From the point of view of the writer, they make it easy to be clear and accurate. But variety in length as well as in type (simple or compound or complex, as classified one way; declarative, imperative, interrogative, or exclamatory, as classified another way) adds to the reader's grasp and retention of what you as the writer are saying to him. Writing that can be read with ease is one achievement; writing that can be read with interest is also an achievement.

Punctuation Possibilities

Varied structure, with its change of pace, keeps the reader alert, at the ready. Even so small a matter as the question mark will signal response. Writers may avail themselves of an interrogative construction, yet fail to follow through with the pay-off, the question mark itself. Less useful in business is the "emotive" exclamation mark; sometimes it sounds hysterical. Another hysterical gesture is overcapitalization. The rule, simply put, is to capitalize the first letter of a sentence, of a proper noun, or of a proper adjective. Capitalizing at random for the purpose of emphasis defeats that purpose.

Varied sentence patterning means that you can use the full range of punctuation symbols, which may be as expressive as words. One mark, the dash, has had such a vogue (perhaps out of uncertainty as to a more exact mark) that it is being worn out. Strictly speaking, it indicates a break in the sentence structure. Loosely speaking, it indicates anything or nothing. Like the boy who cried "Wolf" too often, the writer will find that nothing happens in the mind of his reader from overuse of the dash.

It is possible in one contrived paragraph to illustrate the different punctuation needed when you make different uses of one word. The particular word, "however," loses its differentiations unless properly punctuated:

> The tone in business writing depends on your personality however you look at it. The techniques for special kinds of communications will help you, however, to make your tone ring true. However, no technique can drown out the sound of false or insincere tone. Let's write naturally; however, let's write skillfully too. Unskilled writing may prove meaningless, however natural.

Customs change in regard to punctuation just as they do in regard to word choice, sentence variety, and paragraph length. As in the latter elements, the trend in punctuation is toward simplification. Fewer marks are being used; the writer therefore has to pick and choose so that he does not slow up his reader either by old-fashioned overuse or by experimental underuse.

The comma remains perhaps the most versatile of marks. There are times when it certainly is indispensable, as when its absence or presence determines whether meaning is or is not restricted. "We also tested the arithmetical accuracy of the inventory records," reported an auditor, "and the basis of pricing which was in use during the period was investigated." The auditor needed to make it clear that he investigated only one pricing basis, not any previously used. In other words, the clause, "which was in use during the period," has to be present as a necessary restriction on his meaning. It is a restrictive clause and for that reason is not separated from the rest of the sentence by commas. "The client was requested to give us his co-operation, which we appreciated." Inasmuch as the clause, "which we appreciated," could be dropped from the sentence without making the meaning inaccurate, the comma is needed to set it off. The outcome of certain legal and financial cases has rested upon the rule of punctuation illustrated by these two sentences.

Another comma problem for which there is no one hard and fast answer relates to placing it before "and" introducing the last items in a series:

> He added up the figures, checked the balance, and saw the shortage.

It would be correct to omit the second comma but it is correct—and helpful when the items are not short—to put the comma in. Consistency in policy will save the writer from having to decide each time, though his policy should not be so binding that he can't vary it to fit different kinds of series.

The simple apostrophe is a mark strangely and disastrously subject to omission. It informs the reader of a number of things, chiefly of possession or of contraction. One word involves both uses. "Its" when intended to stand for a noun in the possessive case ("its stockholders") is one exception to the requirement of an apostrophe before the final "s" to show possession. "It's" for "It is" is an example of the requirement of an apostrophe to show the omission of a letter in a contraction.

Not only is an apostrophe needed generally with the final "s" to show possession, but it must stand in the right position: that is, before the final "s" if the word is singular, after if plural. And the difference can run into money as well as other essential matters: "The prior years Federal taxes are the 100 per cent penalty assessment," wrote one tax adjuster. Until an apostrophe is inserted either before or after the "s" in "years," the reader won't know the extent of the penalty.

Precisely used punctuation marks like the semicolon, the comma, and all the rest are essential to meaning. Mistakes both humorous and serious have been made in the interpretation of cablegrams which, for some reason, can be punctuated only by paying for the word "Stop." Look back at the help from the comma in Churchill's seventy-five-word sentence on his wartime career.

Remember also the old conundrum: "Charles the First walked and talked a half an hour after his head was cut off." The solution to this apparent impossibility is as simple as the insertion of a semicolon following "talked" and a comma following "after."

The colon is particularly useful in the strictly structured style of business. It introduces the substantial quotation or enumeration, and it precedes the tabulation upon which we depend for quick coverage of related items.

Abbreviations generally require the period after them, but even with the requisite punctuation they should be used sparingly in formal communication. Since the reader is forced to do the work of filling in what has been left out, abbreviating may be a discourtesy as well as an ambiguity.

Emphasis

Sentences are one of the instruments of emphasis. Whatever stands first and last in a group of words gets primary attention; words placed in the middle are less well remembered. For this reason, sentences are weak in impact when they begin weakly, as does this one. Placing the key words first, as in this sentence, gives those words stress. The approach is head on in the first of these two versions but not in the second:

> Use of a computer should, we believe, be tried.
> We believe that it is worth trying the use of a computer.

The head-on approach makes for fast, definite communication, but overuse can also wear a reader out by throwing too much at him too emphatically too often. Here again, diversity in word order provides reader relief.

Structure built with regard for the end of the sentence as well as the beginning is the means to suspense. Suspense is one way, if sparingly used, to hold your reader. Setting forth data to carry him forward requires you, at the end of the sentence, to repay this attention. Sinclair Lewis, who struggled all his life to wring the full meaning out of words, paid tribute to the deceased father of a friend in one moving sentence:

> Whatever one may write is so blundering, & I can say only that I authentically loved him—not only for his wit, his learning, his immense kindness to me when I was a youngster & broke (that kindness in which you all shared) , and the high standard of honor which he carried so unyieldingly, but most of all for an almost undefinable gracefulness and graciousness & ease which has always instructed me, which very much still does, instruct me, that even when mankind seem heavy and commonplace, they can, a few of them, be as beautifully fine as he was.*

Lewis' emotion is gradually built till the reader is carried by its full momentum to the end. To disavow the long sentence in more mundane matters is to give up one powerful means to our ends.

Only note how the long sentence is being unfolded in

* Quoted in Mark Schorer, *Sinclair Lewis: An American Life* (New York: McGraw-Hill Book Co., 1961) , pp. 158-59.

certain magazines—*The New Yorker,* for instance. Perhaps such syntactical tours de force have a snob appeal of their own. Properly articulated, they are serviceable and effective. They are not easy to write if they are to be made easy to read. Undeniably, the short sentence remains safer for the unpracticed writer.

Sentences that are short have the virtue of being easy to write and easy to read. Longer sentences offer more possibilities for emphasis, climax, interest. They need greater care on the part of the writer in seeing that they are correctly put together, effectively punctuated, judiciously distributed.

The Paragraph

Length

From words grow sentences, and from sentences grow paragraphs. Short, well-knit paragraphs focused on one idea, fact, or incident carry a reader over the ground rapidly. Not only will the reader's eye get relief from frequent space breaks between paragraphs, but his mind will get the sense of accomplishing one thing before going on to the next. A new start is like a fresh grip on the subject. If the reader has grown restive or dubious, a new paragraph offers the possibility of a change for the better. But as with words and with sentences, brevity contains its own doom. There may be monotony; there may be oversimplification; there may be dispersion of thought. Though there is no reason to outlaw one-sentence paragraphs, an excessive number of plays for the reader's attention diminishes pulling power.

Interconnections

You, as the writer, make an implicit promise of progression every time you start a new paragraph. The opening sentence, the lead-in, must furnish accurate indication as to what the paragraph will contain.

The first sentence (usually the topic sentence) should be like an umbrella, big enough to spread over all facts or ideas in the paragraph but no bigger. The sentences in the paragraph should not wander outside the umbrella's protective perimeter, as do these:

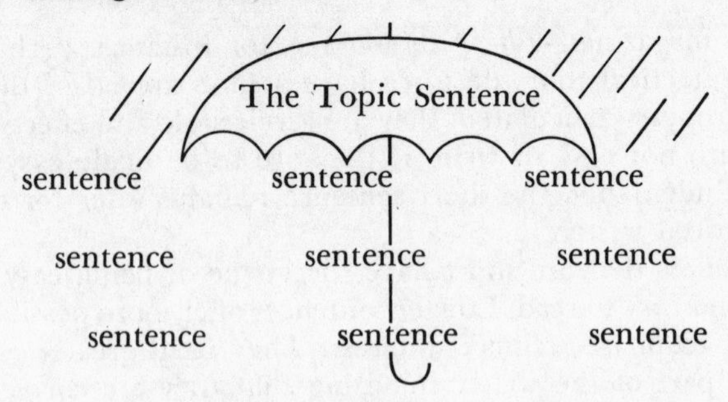

It is equally sensible to make the sentences take full advantage of the umbrella's span. These sentences do not take full advantage:

The Topic Sentence

sentence

sentence

sentence

Not only does the lead-in have a logical function, but it may also serve a psychological purpose in providing transition from what has just preceded. The connection of the upcoming paragraph with the preceding one may at times be self-evident. If so, there is no need to beat the reader over the head by pointing out the connection. At other times it is necessary to be explicit, particularly in technical subject matter, to show how one topic moves to the next. Transitional sentences are those which face both forward and backward. Inevitably they stand near the beginning or end of a paragraph. Often, whole sentences are not needed; mere words or phrases will supply the connection.

In one illustration, a letter addressed to Harry S. Truman in 1944 just after he was elected Vice-President, explicit transitions are spelled out for the sake of fast coverage. A copy of Paderewski's "Minuet" accompanied the letter:

THE UNIVERSITY OF MICHIGAN
William L. Clements Library

November 9, 1944

The Hon. Harry S. Truman
Independence, Missouri

My dear Vice-President-Elect:

If you are going to be associated with our mutual friend Franklin D. Roosevelt, you are going to have to get used to this kind of thing.

The President's real joy in life is his library at Hyde Park. He made me do a lot of work in organizing it.

Now we, at The University of Michigan, have a comparable library of rarities. In our collections are autographs of prominent Americans, from Christopher Columbus to the present time.

We want yours for our collection.

If there is any truth in that story about your playing Paderewski's Minuet at the Muehlebach while everyone else was jittery about the election returns, what more appropriate than that you give us your autograph on the enclosed?

If your secretary tries to ditch this, I'm going after Bob Hannegan; if he fails, I'm going to ask the President to intercede for me—and I know you would not want to have us take up the President's time, now, would you?

Very truly yours,

(Signed) Randolph G. Adams
Director

/dr
Enclosure

You can pick out, word for word, the connecting links between the rapid-fire paragraphs: President, library, collection, autograph. (The Clements Library got the autograph as requested.)

Emphasis

If emphasis is worth watching in sentence structure, it is doubly so in the more extensive unit of the paragraph. Put first or last what you want remembered most. What appears in between will get less notice, a point worth knowing when there is negative or unwelcome material to include. You can present material vigorously; you can present material gently; but to do so means knowing how to control emphasis.

Paragraphs as "Carriers"

Tense jumping. Paragraphs can be the carriers of certain ills common to everyday writing. Tenses may jump when no jump in time is involved. Though tense jumping is easy to do by mistake, Hersey gives us a shock in the opening of *Hiroshima* by a blatant and intentional jump from past to present: "Hiroshima was a fan-shaped city, lying mostly on the six islands . . . A rim of mountains runs around the other three sides of the delta. Though the old city is gone, the mountains remain."

Person switching. Paragraphs which jump unwarrantedly from the first, second, or third person are faulty. You, as the writer, need to take up a position, to find your voice at the outset, and to speak throughout in that voice. Only then will the reader know the point of view from which you are speaking. Some writers inadvertently start with the first person, switch to the third, and end up with the second: "Until now I have not been aware of the many alternatives one can consider before finally selecting the most appropriate word you can use." The reader loses his bearings by such switching. Of course, pronouns of all three persons may appear in the same context without constituting unwarranted switching.

Using personal pronouns adds color and life, though in formal business reports the impersonal third person is still the more common. Hesitancy of the writer to speak as "I" and resistance of the reader to anything but the corporate voice accounts for the detachment, dry as it is. Talking directly to the reader, to "you," through use of the second person, holds attention, but it needs to be done from the start. Whatever person you choose, be consistent about reference to personal pronouns. Adopt a position at the outset and hold to it, so that the reader does not suddenly find himself, near the end, being directly addressed as "you" for the first time or being instructed in the imperative mood: "Check procedures."

Antecedent dropping. Pronouns which lose their antecedents between paragraphs mystify the reader. Of all the word traps, "this"—the demonstrative pronoun—is the worst: "You may have to try many a suggestion before arriving at the most profitable solution. I offer you this one below." (Suggestion or solution?) What "this" stands for may be known to you as the writer when you use it, but even you may have trouble later in tracing the specific object or the vague concept for which it was meant to stand. "This" frequently characterizes lazy, take-it-for-granted communication, and "these" and "those" are words liable to the same misuse.

Reference to vague, remote, buried, or lost antecedents by any kind of pronoun is a habit worth curing. The cure takes conscious effort and correction. A management consultant wrote: "We appreciate the advantages of taking in an outside stockholder which will minimize the financial risk." If "which" refers to "stockholder" it should be changed to "who." If "which" refers to "advantages" the pronoun should not be so far away.

A tax man wrote: "His illness and long period of unemployment made it necessary for him to withdraw all funds which he had accumulated to pay hospital and doctor bills." Does the relative pronoun "which" refer back to "all funds"? Or only to funds accumulated for one purpose? The manager of a utility office tried to explain the system he followed: "Since the meters are inside consumers' buildings, the reader leaves a card for the consumer to fill out when he is unable to enter." The noun standing closest to the personal pronoun "he" is "consumer," and the closest noun is expected to be the antecedent. But "he," of course, stands for the "reader." Only a Henry James should play at the game of hide-and-seek with antecedents. Ambiguity is seldom the intent, though often the defect, of functional writing.

Action killing. Paragraphs with verbs preponderantly passive go dead on their feet. Making your subject the receiver of the action (passive voice) instead of the doer (active voice) takes away the sense of action, the feeling of movement. There are times to take the onus off the subject as in the question, "The document was lost?" instead of "You lost the document?" But paragraphs with plenty of the active voice are most likely to make a direct, forceful impression.

Number changing. Fundamental to a reader is the knowledge of how many persons, places, or things you are discussing at one time (in one paragraph, for instance). Is it one thing or more? The only way you can keep a subject clear between yourself and your reader is to write consistently. The reader is naturally confused by a statement like this one: "Customers pleased with the interest of the Company and dealer will be more likely to return to that dealer when service work is required on their car." Since this writer is talking about more than one customer, he should refer to more than one car. Agreement is the rule at stake here, and agreement in number applies as between subject and verb, between noun and pronoun, between such obviously related words as the excerpt contains.

A common mistake in agreement (as in "Each location prepares their budgets") arises from failure to recognize that words like "each," "every," "either" are singular. The habitual treatment of collective nouns like "management," "personnel" and "company" as plural is at least awkward and, in the eyes of some, incorrect: "Management depends on the salesmen as their primary contact with the customer." In this sentence the pronoun "their" was intended to refer back to "management." As a collective noun, management has a singular sense for many, as the verb in the singular shows. The plural pronoun confuses such readers, especially when a *bona fide* plural noun ("salesmen") stands closer to the pronoun than the actual antecedent, "management."

"Should a company be treated in the singular or plural sense?" wrote one frustrated secretary of a top executive. The confusion extended beyond the collective noun itself to the actual name of the organization: "I'd like to know the accepted treatment when referring to a company . . . There seems to be a widespread inconsistency in this usage." Then she listed among her recent problems:

	This?	Or this?
1.	Dow's products . . .	Dows' products . . .
2.	Champlain-Zapatta does have . . .	Champlain-Zapatta do have . . .
3.	United Fruit and its proposal . . .	United Fruit and their proposal . . .

In each of the three instances the wording in the left column seems preferable.

A paragraph or series of paragraphs which switches back and forth in the number of the noun or pronoun (i.e., singular or plural) is not going to make sense to a reader. Making sense is the real reason for following the rules of agreement.

Basic Ingredients of Style

Churchill, in describing how he learned to write as a young man, commented on just what we have been considering:

> I began to see that writing . . . was not only an affair of sentences, but of paragraphs. Indeed I thought the paragraph no less important than the sentence . . . Just as the sentence contains one idea in all its fullness, so the paragraph should embrace a distinct episode; and as sentences should follow one another in harmonious sequence, so the paragraphs must fit on to one another like the automatic couplings of railway carriages.

Paragraphs, like sentences and like words themselves, cannot be measured by the mere matter of length. Shortness is productive of quick understanding. But monotony can be avoided only by variation. Emphasis, too, requires some space to develop. Knowing the powers, magical or not, of the three basic units of language—the word, the sentence, the paragraph—is the only way you can deliver the multiple messages of modern business. These units are the seeds of style. Style is something which everyone who puts pen to paper possesses. It may or may not be good style, but it is the intangible quality which distinguishes the writing of one person from that of the next.

4: Planning Form

Aristotle in describing the relation between "form" and "matter" in the universe represented it as a copper bowl. The design (or form) of the bowl is inconceivable without thinking of the copper substance (or matter) of which the bowl is shaped.

In writing, you choose the form that fits your subject matter, and in the fit or suitability lies your success or failure. Form is no more fixed and limited for a piece of written matter than for a bowl or any other object of creation. And writing—whether for business, for the stage, or for any other purpose—is creative.

Forms Current in Business

Business will need more forms of written communication than all those now known, such as the formal report, letter report, memo, letter, directive, telegram, specifications, job procedure, computer program, instructions, analysis, position paper, questionnaire, speech, release, professional article, advertisement, script, digest, budget, routing slip. These are among the communications most familiar to businessmen. Originally, each was designed to fit some particular matter in hand at the moment.

Other forms besides those mentioned are sure to be originated, and the old forms are being readapted every day. For instance, accountants have become accustomed to definite forms for audit reports. The profession of accounting has, in fact, prescribed certain forms like the short-form audit report. Now, however, some accounting firms find themselves engaged in writing a different sort of report: the management service report. The inclination is to carry over the old form of report as being familiar and trustworthy, whether it is the form most suitable for the non-audit client or not. New forms, departing from the old, are being tried gradually. Out of necessity comes invention. Forms have to be developed and redeveloped because the copper of business life changes. The shape of its written expression must change accordingly.

The businessman who writes cannot stop at being a report writer. When the famous young man in the gray flannel suit was applying for a new job in Rockefeller Plaza, the executive interviewing him demanded: "Can you write?" Tom, having replied that on his present job the annual report to the trustees was his responsibility, was then asked to compose, in the next hour, his autobiography. "Write anything you want, but at the end of your last page," he was ordered, "I'd like you to finish the sentence: 'The most significant fact about me is . . .' "

Tom, left alone, tried to write as directed. After an agonizing interval, he concluded his brief paragraph with this: "I have decided that I do not wish to attempt an autobiography as part of an application for a job."

In the story that follows, Tom's decision on the matter of the autobiography provides the key. For the moment, we can put his refusal down to a question of the suitability of form to matter. What counts is a sense of distinction, the ability to determine what goes with what. A budding personnel specialist was assigned to trace down a difficulty in over-the-counter negotiations between a utility company and a consumer. After interviewing all the parties involved, the personnel man submitted the record to the district manager in a question-and-answer form. It read with the ease of a dramatic script in which the hero and the villain were left to disclose themselves.

The need in choosing your form is for flexibility, even for originality. Sometimes standardization helps your reader; if he receives data from you periodically in the same way, his time is saved because he knows where to look for what he needs to know.

Format for a Long Report

Every form of communication has its own features, the familiarity of which is a convenience to reader and writer both. Particular companies develop particular forms which, because they are well known to reader and writer, save the time of both. Let us first take the form which in business is perhaps the most formal and complete of those in common use. The features of the formal report, represented for you in what follows, speak for themselves. Any one form, like the formal report, consists of special parts, each individually identifiable.

(Title Page)

FORMAT FOR A LONG REPORT

Prepared for Businessmen

by
Report Writer

THE UNIVERSITY OF MICHIGAN
Graduate School of Business
Administration
Ann Arbor, Michigan
date

(Letter of Transmittal)

The University of Michigan
Graduate School of
Business Administration
Ann Arbor, Michigan
June 2, 196_

Businessmen Who Write
Offices, Plants, Stores
U. S. A.
Gentlemen:

A report on a report is what I am transmitting to you here. You need to have in concise shape certain information on the technical parts used in report writing.

For that reason, I am reporting to you about the format for the long report.

Please notice the discussion of where a report writer places any recommendations he has to make. Business is using the "head-on" approach more and more, for reasons you will find obvious, I think.

Questions that occur to you about the FORMAT FOR A LONG REPORT may be considered in more detail by us later.

Yours sincerely,

(Signed)

RW/jfc
Report Writer
Enclosure

(Table of Contents)

CONTENTS

I. Introduction

Apart from its content, a major report stands or falls upon the way it is presented. Its setup or format is a controlling factor in its success.

For the writer who wishes to take advantage of familiar and sensible design, certain definite parts are available for use.

Some long reports contain between their covers all the formal parts; other long reports contain some of them. The individual writer has to be selective, deciding what he needs each time he makes a report. The parts most frequently employed in business today are: title page, letter of authorization, letter of transmittal, table of contents, table of exhibits, synopsis, introduction, body, end section, recommendations, appendix, bibliography.

II. Basis for Designing Format

In choosing the parts to incorporate in a formal report,

(1)

the writer has to ask himself two questions:

Am I merely giving information, or am I also making recommendations?

What setup will be most helpful to my reader in grasping my subject?

The parts chosen for inclusion should be based on whether the report is "informational" or "analytical," and whether the reader needs the full range of parts.

Other guide questions can be usefully asked by the writer of himself at the outset (see Appendix).

As well as asking himself the two essential questions given, the report writer needs to know what each part can and cannot do.

III. Survey of Separate Parts

In business, reports use certain parts more than others. An index, for instance,is seldom necessary, or a preface. Of the parts described some, like the title page, are indispensable.

(2)

A. The title page shows the exact subject of the report in brief, accurate, and interesting wording. It also shows the person(s) for whom it is intended, the name of the writer(s), and sometimes the position(s) held. The company or institution, the city, and the date of its origin are given. Without a title page, a report lacks a face. The document when filed will be a mystery. With a title page, the report speaks for itself as a self-evident document.

B. The letter of authorization, though not so often used nowadays, is from the individual wishing the report to inform the person who is to write it as to what is wanted. A specific letter of authorization may ensure getting certain answers, may prevent confusion and unnecessary work, and may set limits on time and length.

C. The letter (or memo) of transmittal, often used, is from the writer to the reader (or authorizer) saying, in substance: "Here is the report you re-

(3)

quested." The letter of transmittal in a direct, quick beginning, may refresh the reader's memory as to the reason for the report, acknowledge any special help received in the writing of it, and call the reader's attention to items of peculiar interest. Any special difficulties that were encountered in preparing the material may also be mentioned. When a report is formally worded in the third person, the informal use of the first and second is possible only here in the transmittal communication. As a letter, this part permits a person-to-person tone not elsewhere customary in a formal report. It affords the opportunity of a personal signature, a more valuable addition than is sometimes recognized.

D. The table of contents, on a page headed as such, lists the section (or chapter) headings with their page references. Graduated indention may be used to distinguish the divisions and subdivisions. Though very formal reports use Arabic numerals for the report proper and small Roman numerals for prefatory and appended pages, Arabic numerals are often used throughout. The headings appear just as they do within the report itself, expressed in parallel structure. For instance:

not

The table of contents may give merely main headings (like a skeleton outline), or it may include subheadings as well (like an annotated preview). The reader in either case gets a survey of the total presentation. Though the table of contents often adheres to the outline prepared before the report is written, it should not be put in final form till afterward. The letter of transmittal and the synopsis should be listed unless the author expects them to be detached for separate distribution.

(5)

E. The table of exhibits, used when there are a number of them, is set up at the beginning like the table of contents, though headed separately. It lists by name and page such graphic aids as charts, diagrams, tables, maps, drawings, and photos.

F. The synopsis, labeled as such and preferably limited to one page, gives a bird's-eye view of the entire report. Even though the rest of the report is double spaced this section may be single spaced. It is not a review or commentary on the report. Often requested by publishers on book manuscripts, the statement may be used for independent purposes. The same sequence followed in the full report is followed in the synopsis with the same balance and emphasis. There should be no new material which has not been presented in the report proper. Room is usually lacking for headings. Short paragraphs are helpful. They can sometimes be built from restatement of topic sentences of key paragraphs.

(6)

Rarely if ever should graphics be incorporated. Only major points can, of course, be covered, but one or two pieces of factual evidence are needed as well as the conclusions to indicate that evidence <u>is</u> used in the report proper. When a writer is going to present his recommendations at the opening of the report, a synopsis may be less necessary. Likewise, when the recommendations may initially be unacceptable to the reader, a synopsis may be inadvisable. In the latter circumstance the letter of transmittal can be made to serve the partial purpose of a synopsis. This particular part (also called abstract, brief, résumé, summary, précis, highlights) may be the only part of a long report that some readers take time to see. The acid test to which a writer must put his synopsis is this: "<u>If</u> my reader goes no further, am I content to let my report stand on the synopsis?"

(7)

G. The introduction, which opens the report itself, is a make-or-break point. It states and defines the subject directly, points out the issue (if any) to be solved, gives background or history, sets the limits or scope of coverage, and—as transition into the body—explains the plan of presentation. This plan of presentation (methodology) consists of the approach, the "attack" to be followed. It tells the reader in advance how the writer has organized his material, and so permits easier reading. Stating the procedure at the end of the introduction clues the reader in on what is coming and the order in which it is coming. He gets a little road map to guide him on his way. In a long report which is divided into sections, each section needs its own introductory statement before the first subsection. Internal introductions of this kind need to follow the same pattern of coverage as the major introduction.

(8)

In addition, the internal introduction may serve one other purpose: transition. It ties the section which it introduces to the section it follows. If all this sounds lengthy and complex, carrying it out need not be.

H. The body, as the longest portion of the report, is itself divided by headings into sections of balanced length and weight. Each section, as has been seen, may have its own introductory and concluding paragraphs. The transition between sections should either be explicit or clearly implicit. The headings themselves help with transition.

I. The end section, like the introduction, stands in a spot of inevitable emphasis. To every organized presentation there naturally has to be a beginning, a middle, and an end. The end section may do all or some of three things: (1) summarize by factual recapitulation, (2) draw conclusions by putting to-

(9)

gether and adding up the facts, (3) recommend action. A report in which the final section consists of new subject matter seems to stop short. The reader may be left hanging in the air.

The chance to draw material together for the sake of clarity and emphasis at the end of a report is also available at the end of each section in a long report. Internal summaries, interspersed as the reader progresses, reinforce his understanding. In the last analysis, the writer then prepares a summary of summaries.

J. The appendix, headed as a separate part at the end of the report, is the place to put data or documents used as source material, or supplementary data. It is not always necessary, but if used, appended material should be referred to in the course of the report proper. It really affords the writer a chance to back up what he says with further evidence.

(10)

K. The bibliography, which differs from footnotes or citations given on individual pages, is a systematic listing of published sources used by the writer or related generally to the subject. Each listing should include the name of the author spelled in full or with initials, the title of the book or article, and the date and place of publication. Sometimes the name of the publisher is given. A bibliography may be divided into groups by books, pamphlets, newspapers, and any types of written sources used. It may also carry the writer's notations on each listing. Business depends less often on bibliographical sources than it does on other materials.

In the preceding survey of the separate parts that may be used in formal reports, the order in which they appear in a report has been followed. An important decision has to be made, however, in regard to the placing of the recommendations.

(11)

IV. Position of the Recommendations

A report that goes beyond being purely informative usually includes a decision or recommendation. This step amounts to proposing a solution, giving an opinion, or suggesting a program of action.

The logically minded writer arrives at his recommendations only after developing his evidence. But the reader—in business a person without time to spare—often wants to get to the decisive part right away. So, using the deductive method, the end result may be stated in the introduction with the supporting evidence to follow in the body. When the recommendations are placed in the introduction, the end section then consists of summary and conclusions. Businessmen increasingly favor this head-on approach.

If, on the other hand, the inductive method is chosen, the writer lets the presentation of his recommendations wait till after he develops his evidence. The end section in that case contains all three elements:

(12)

summary, conclusions, and recommendations.

Since a report that includes recommendations does all three of these things somewhere, either at the beginning or end, the placing of the recommendations and their relationship to the summary and conclusions may be illustrated by a circle (see page 15). The important thing to remember is that the recommendations, whether put first or last, should arise logically out of the conclusions, which themselves are drawn from the summary of facts. A logical report has to come full circle.

V. Conclusion

In designing the format of a long report, businessmen use conventional parts to speed readers on their way. Their readers know what to look for and where they expect to find it. Since the scope of business is itself never fixed, flexibility in design is necessary for business reporting.

Even in the simplest form of communication, repetition will

occur in the first and last spots if nowhere else. In a more elaborate report, the table of contents, the synopsis, the introduction, and the end section cannot avoid repeating. Repetition keeps the reader on the track. "Iterations are commonly loss of time," observed that canny man of affairs, Sir Francis Bacon, centuries ago. "But there is no such gain of time as to iterate often the state of the question."* Though repeating the content is advantageous, wording need not, should not, be the same each time.

The writer has to choose the design that will enable him to discuss the question he has under consideration, to report his data (and recommendations) most succinctly. His choice of form is made with his reader present in his mind's eye.

*Clark S. Northrup, ed., The Essays of Francis Bacon (Boston: Houghton Mifflin Company, 1908), p. 78. (See also modernized version: Essays of Francis Bacon. (New York: Doubleday Dolphin Book, n.d. Paperback.)

(14)

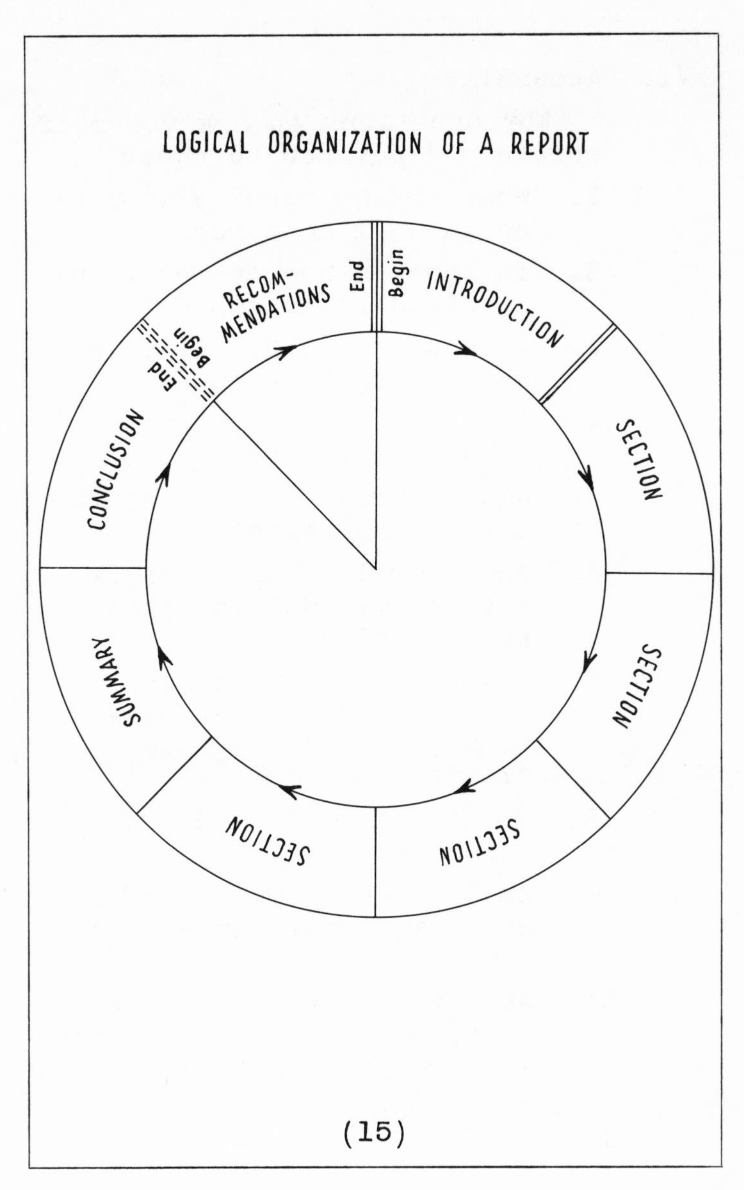
LOGICAL ORGANIZATION OF A REPORT
End
Begin
INTRODUCTION
SECTION
SECTION
SECTION
SECTION
SUMMARY
CONCLUSION
End
Begin
RECOM-
MENDATIONS
(15)

VI. Appendix

Key questions to ask yourself before you put pen to paper:

1. What is the precise subject on which I am reporting?
2. Is there a problem or issue involved in my subject?
3. To whom, specifically, am I addressing this report?
4. Am I writing in my own name or on behalf of a group?
5. What sources am I going to use for my facts?
6. Where am I going to place the recommendations that are called for?
7. Does the situation permit use of the personal pronouns, "I" or "We" and "You"?
8. Is it better to write impersonally?
9. Am I dividing my material so that it will appear in a logical sequence?
10. What formal parts of report writing are needed—for instance, the synopsis?

(16)

Format for a Memo

The long report is a form for the upper levels of management and for matters of major substance. It is not the most frequent form. The short form called the memo or memorandum is relied upon extensively and is second nature to many businessmen for internal circulation. Less often it is sent to outsiders. The tone may be less formal, and the content may assume familiarity with background and terminology as between writer and reader. In spite of differences in length and tone, much that is useful in the longer form holds true for the shorter form of the memo.

The subject line in a memo, for instance, is like the title of the long report: it needs to be accurate, short, and—if not at the expense of those two qualities—interesting. There is no title page or table of contents, of course. An introduction is essential and serves the same purpose as in the longer form though in telescoped style. It identifies the subject with possible reference to background and limitation of scope. To be told in an introduction how the message is going to be presented—its sequence—is as much help to the memo reader as to the reader of the long report. Instead of chapters or separate sections, short paragraphs distinguish the component elements of a memo.

Brief headings, kept parallel in structure and content, speed up intake, even within a one-page memorandum. Another point about headings: in the first sentence that follows the heading the reader should not be made to refer back to the heading to get the meaning. Note how easy it is to avoid making the reader go through that chore:

Reader does the work:

Heading:	*Survey of Job Descriptions*
First sentence of paragraph:	These are essential for internal control and operating efficiency.

Writer does the work instead:	
Heading:	*Survey of Job Descriptions*
First sentence of paragraph:	For internal control and operating efficiency, job descriptions are essential.

Though the second version requires one additional word, the reader's time is saved. Brevity has to be measured by time as well as space.

Brevity is the soul of the memo form. To hold down your total length, you need selectivity, organization, and clarity. You have an initial responsibility to gather all the data pertinent to your problem, but you also have a secondary responsibility to use only so much of it as your reader needs. Further, you have a responsibility to organize and express the data and conclusions in a way logically and psychologically acceptable to your reader. As an illustration, here is a memo on the art of dictating.

June 2, 196_

To: Businessmen Who Write
From: (Mrs.) Mary C. Bromage
Subject: Dictating

Your Setting

If you have business communications to dictate, use simple ways of getting your best results. First, make sure that both you and the secretary have comfortable places to sit, preferably somewhere you are accustomed to sitting. If you are using a dictaphone or other mechanical means, just be sure that you are comfortably settled. Don't try to dictate in short, spasmodic snatches. Sometimes the best intervals are found while traveling. You will need to arrange in order all the letters you are answering. The complex ones may be annotated in the margin with what you want to say.

Give instructions, if possible, when dictating in your own office, that you do not wish to be interrupted by people coming to the door or by telephone calls. Interruptions are extravagant, and besides neither you nor a secretary can do two things at once. One advantage in using a machine is that you can switch it on and off as need be, playing back to pick up your thread of thought.

Your State of Mind

So much for the setting. What about the best frame of mind for dictating? Forget whatever you were doing just before tending to your correspondence, whether it was plans made at the breakfast table or in the elevator on the way up to your office. Focus your thoughts and imagination on the person to whom you are writing. Try to see your reader in your mind's eye; visualize the facial reactions you think your words will produce.

Deciding the purpose to be accomplished in the particular letter is the lion's share of the work. Do that first. Decide not only whether you are going to say "Yes," "No," or "Maybe," but think how you are going to do this. You need to have in mind the order, roughly, in which you will make the necessary points. Do not start talking till your own mind is made up.

Your Reader

Think of the person to whom your letter is going and what he is expecting to hear from you. Unless you can see this individual, your letter may not strike home.

Suppose, then, that you are all

set behind your desk; that you see clearly the recipient; and that, using your notes to follow your predetermined line of reasoning, you start talking your answer.

Your Message

Be sure to name the individual at the outset to whom you are writing, giving the address unless the transcribing secretary has this information. The correct spelling of anyone's name is the first step in communicating with him.

Then start talking as if you were face to face. One of the advantages you gain by dictating rather than writing out your letters yourself is a natural, conversational tone. If you use unfamiliar expressions, foreign terms, or names of persons and places you will usually need to spell them.

But do not let yourself run on just because it is easy to keep talking. You are even more likely to ramble with a machine because it cannot act bored or impatient or give you black looks. Not only does your secretary have to transcribe everything you say, but somebody on the receiving end has to read it all. Pause. Think to yourself rather than out loud with your reader.

Do you want a copy or copies of what you are dictating sent to others? Should those receiving copies be listed or should your secretary make "blind" carbons? Do you want to send your letter airmail? Don't forget necessary instructions.

Your Voice

What about your manner of talking? Two things are important: tone and pace. As for tone, you should speak more clearly than is normal if you are using a dictaphone, because the secretary will not be able to watch as you talk. Therefore, enunciate each syllable and keep your inflection up. Tension and fatigue may creep in to reduce the smooth, even flow which is, of course, most serviceable. Stress the ends of sentences, clauses, phrases, and the last letters of words themselves. If you picture yourself on a stage trying to project your voice to the last row in the second balcony, you will get an idea of clarity—although you need not speak loudly.

And what about pace? This depends on the experience of your secretary if she is taking it in shorthand. With a machine, she can control the speed. Some secretaries prefer that you speak as fast as in regular conversation; others will appreciate unusual deliberateness. Regardless of how fast you yourself can think and talk, change your inflection to indicate where commas and periods belong.

Most secretaries put in the correct punctuation for standard usage. If what you are saying calls for unusual punctuation (quotation marks, dashes, exclamation points), you must dictate them, dropping your voice so that the word "dash" does not appear in the letter but just the mark itself. Say "paragraph" to indicate where a new one begins; your secretary has no way of knowing how your thoughts are going to develop and cannot help you out in this respect.

If you use your voice to group your words, and if you phrase according to the natural sense of what you are saying, your secretary will be able to follow your meaning. Think of how a crooner "phrases" what he sings to put his words across.

So just be sure that you think through your letter before you start. Settle yourself with some sense of relaxation. Keep your mind on what you are doing instead of what you may wish you were doing. Use a clear, emphatic voice. And remember that your secretary cannot be expected to supply paragraphing or unusual spelling and punctuation.

One more thing. No matter how many letters you have on your mind to write, stop before you reach the point of rambling. There is a tendency, particularly in difficult messages, to keep talking even after all has been said. The end of what you have to say may be reached before you realize it.

Mary C. Bromage

Mary C. Bromage

MCB/jfc

Format for a Letter Report

A report, whether long or short, whether a formal one or merely a memo, usually stresses the logical approach. A letter is apt to stress the psychological approach. The form which combines features of both the report and the letter is known as the letter report. The organization of the letter report emphasizes the logical approach by the use of an identifying introduction, headings for the midpart, and a summary at the end. The appearance of the letter report emphasizes the psychological approach because of the salutation and complimentary close.

The value of this particular format is that your presentation can be more substantial and more systematic than in the usual letter. At the same time, your tone can be more personal and informal than in the usual report. Suggestions for reading *Hiroshima* form the subject of a sample letter report.

Graduate School of Business
  Administration
The University of Michigan
Ann Arbor, Michigan
June 2, 196_

Businessmen Who Write
Offices, Plants, Stores
U.S.A.

Gentlemen:

Reading the work of good authors, whether fact or fiction, can give you ideas for writing reports and letters. The basic principles hold true for different kinds of writing: organization, economy, clarity, consideration of the reader.

Although the subject of John Hersey's HIROSHIMA is not light reading, this factual report offers some discoveries for those who have to write.

You will discover for yourself much of its applicability, but this is a "letter report" with my suggestions for studying this book—and, later, other books.

Taking Notes

As you read HIROSHIMA, have a pencil in hand. Why not use the margins and flyleaves for your reactions as you go along?

1. List the characters by name, occupation, age, address, family, income.
2. Locate the individual characters at the time of the explosion.
3. Observe what each did when the bomb hit.
4. List dates with identifying happenings.
5. Note the chapter titles.

<u>Raising Questions</u>

In addition to certain questions about the subject which I am suggesting, others may occur to you to bring up.

1. What is the author's subject?
2. How did he organize the presentation of his subject? What purpose does the chapter division serve?
3. Would you call this piece of writing a story? A report? A news account?
4. From what point of view is the author writing? Is the first person pronoun used? Is he writing in retrospect?
5. What factors are employed to unify the account? Are there parallel observations on each character?

6. Is there a time sequence?
7. Is the report based on fact? Inference?
8. Why did the author begin the way he did?

Relation of Reading to Writing

What, after all, has reading to do with writing? And what has such a publication as HIROSHIMA to offer a man writing business communications? Style is a many-splendored thing—sometimes short and sweet; sometimes long and analytical; always, however, adapted to its intended "consumer" and always sufficient unto its subject and purpose. Good authors provide us with models for various kinds of writing.

In giving you a specific title and author, I have a definite purpose. To write well you need to keep in mind those who are professional in this field. Writers like the one discussed here, who has won many readers, have adapted their use of words to the subjects they have in mind and have considered how best to appeal to their readers.

You yourselves probably have different purposes, different subjects, different readers. The principles of selectivity and of adaptation remain valid for everyone who writes.

Sincerely yours,

Mary C. Bromage

(Mrs.) Mary C. Bromage
Asst. Professor of Written
Communication

MCB/jfc

5: Organizing Content To Fit Purpose

The circumstances surrounding anything to be written are your first consideration as writer. The situation or circumstances cover a multitude of vital points such as your relationship to your reader, to your subject, to your purpose.

The style in which you word your communication is your next consideration. The form in which you cast your material certainly follows. By now you are well into the undertaking; you must at once arrange your material or be engulfed by it.

Organizing, for the methodically minded, is a game to play with pleasure. For others, it may become a revelation. Those most methodically minded need to be careful that organization does not become the master, distorting the end result. The less methodically minded must not leave to the reader the job of creating order out of chaos. Organization, as we shall interpret the term, means the order in which the points of a communication are presented: the one-two-three sequence of paragraphs, sections, or chapters.

The best organization, whether in a novel or a business report, a sermon or a poem, may be expounded in advance or may be made to speak for itself. It should never be obtrusive or pedantic. To ask a reader to follow you without telling him where he is going or how he is going to get there is like asking someone to start on a journey to an unknown place without telling him the means of transportation.

Relation of Form to Organization

Once principles of communicability are recognized—the principle, for instance, of announcing your subject and the principle of summing it up—form can be adapted, reshaped, molded, to fit the subject and the situation. Time may be saved both for you and for your reader if you take advantage of conventions as to appearance (form). Not always does familiarity breed contempt; rather, it often breeds satisfaction in the reader.

In the business letter, as an age-old form, the reader expects to find certain items in certain spots. If his name and address as the receiver are not just above the salutation (as they sometimes are not today), he continues looking for them till he finds them, maybe at the bottom. The one element of form indispensable, all but immovable in a letter, is the personal signature. And when it has to be a rubber stamp, you can be sure your reader will be holding it up to the light or under the magnifying glass to catch you. Reader expectations are not to be treated lightly in matters of form.

The success of any message lies partly in how it looks at first glance, in a familiar or pleasing form to catch the eye. Appearance can change superficially, is constantly changing, as a matter of fact. To all such changes, the reader must be reconditioned. Change for the sake of change is a waste, but when the contact can be more quickly and clearly established by some new device, business does not hesitate to change.

Whatever the form, visibility is a necessity. The form you choose may be a letter for its person-to-person tone, a memo for its assumption of common ground, a formal report for its dignity and capaciousness, or perhaps something as different as a news release with its triple spacing. Visibility is the reader's first inducement, and it is that which memorializes John Hancock to this day above the other signers of the Declaration of Independence. White space, color when possible, graphic illustrations that range from folding charts to mere arrows that point on a page are among the means to visibility which are at your command. Tabulation, underlining, reasonable capitalizing, varied indention—these are useful accompaniments of form.

Humpty Dumpty occupied himself with the question of mastery in communicating—the question of the word versus meaning. As between form and content, there can be no doubt as to which is master: the content dictates the form. The design you choose for your message depends upon what you have to say.

Basic Patterns

Organization is so basic to logical thinking that it is easy to put a finger on certain universal ways of achieving it. Time and space are usually the guiding factors. You may present your material in a time sequence, telling what happened first, next, and so on to the end: a simple chronology. A variation of the chronological method is the flashback, in which you state first the current problem or crisis, then fill in on all that has led up to it, and go on from there to subsequent developments. Or you may present your material in the dimension of space. This means that you tell what the situation is in one place, what it is in another, and another till you have a panorama. A third fundamental approach is the pro-and-con presentation. Here, the strong points or assets or advantages may be shown on the one hand, and the weak points or liabilities or disadvantages on the other, in comparative fashion. Still a fourth pattern in business reporting is the functional one, in which the reader is given, say, the purchasing department first, then personnel, shipping, and so on.

The twists and turns that can be given the underlying, organizational schemes of time, space, comparison, and function are as various as the ingenuity of authors. Chaucer, in the Prologue to *The Canterbury Tales,* put into the mouth of his tavernkeeper an elaborate plan, based on both time and space. Each pilgrim, riding in that goodly company to the shrine of St. Thomas à Becket, was to pass the time by telling four stories, two on the way to Canterbury, two more coming back. Then the particular pilgrim

> . . . that telleth in this caas
> Tales of best sentence and moost solaas

was to be wined and dined on the return trip at mine host's inn as a reward and farewell celebration.

Though Chaucer never fully completed the undertaking, what he did carry out was made clear for readers throughout the centuries. Each section of this great work was given its own caption: "Heere Bigynneth the Knyghtes Tale," "Heere Bigynneth the Monkes Tale," for instance.

The headings of an outline may be transferred, if parallel in structure and in content, from the outline to the report. Such headings may be used not only for your table of contents but also throughoutout the pages of the report itself. By distributing them in the proper places and placing them with consistent differentiation (center or side, capitalized or not, underlined or not) the reader gets route markers to guide him.

Every organized project, whether it is a journey, a piece of writing, or a ball game, proceeds according to a plan, the upshot having to arise out of the plan. "The progression in ideas, which is true method, starts from a rightly chosen initiative," argued the poet and philosopher, Samuel Taylor Coleridge. A report like every other activity has to have a beginning, a middle, and an end. Further, the end must be contained in the beginning. Organization elicits unity, if it does justice to the material. Just what the organizational sequence is should not normally be kept a mystery.

Writers in outlining their reports cannot take too much for granted as to the reader's ability to guess at the way the data are to be unfolded. Chaucer spelled his method out for his readers. So, too, do some of the most readable reports in business. Mechanical wording has to be avoided in doing so. Unless the introduction provides information on the sequence that is to come, reading it will be like trying to pin the tail on the donkey while you are blindfolded.

Emphasis

Your subject matter is not the only factor to take into account in planning organization. Consider your reader in selecting the avenue of approach. Organization produces built-in, automatic emphasis. What you put at the beginning and the end is likely to prove most influential. You recall the old adage, "He who laughs last laughs best." With the principle of emphasis in mind, you can make your decisions as to where you put recommendations you may be making. Sir Francis Bacon, centuries ago, made use of a trick sometimes thought the invention of Madison Avenue: "I knew one," wrote this wily statesman and financier, "that, when he wrote a letter, he would put that which was most material in the postscript, as if it had been a by-matter." What catches the eye last is certainly apt to linger in the mind. But what catches the eye first may determine whether the reader ever gets as far as the end.

In a deductively organized report, the recommendation (conclusion, opinion, solution, call it by whatever name) comes in the initial section. As the writer, you will, of course, arrive at this point only after weighing the evidence first. But having worked your way through by the deliberate, logical consideration of the pros and cons, you can then give your reader the benefit of the quick answer. You will still have to follow up with all the data and alternatives and reasons that convinced you of the position you have taken in your opening.

When Eisenhower was in the White House, his report writers were under instructions to present a decision, even to propose a course of action executing the decision, first. Placing his confidence in his staff, President Eisenhower would not necessarily have to work his own way through all the supporting data. President Kennedy, on the other hand, was often described as passing over any opening conclusion to wade through the supporting material in a report, and only then to be prepared to consider a recommendation. Readers differ. Writers must make their reports differ accordingly. The situation is the controlling element.

When the end of a report contains the recommendation, in accordance with the inductive scheme of organization, this arrangement makes for a slower reaction. However, it may be more persuasive if the reader is not predisposed to accept what is being recommended. The choice as between beginning and end was pungently put by the late

Mike Todd when visited, as frequently he was, by persons soliciting money. His answer often was: "How do you want your 'No'? Fast or slow?" With the public's increasing awareness of its own psychological nature, its hypersophistication, the effect of the slow "No," of explanations first and then the negative answer, has been undercut.

In reporting the Hiroshima story, John Hersey did not have the problem of a final opinion or a thesis and its acceptability or unacceptability. He simply recounted what happened to six residents of that city at set periods of time. The organizational scheme, in spite of his impressionistic chapter headings, is chronology, but chronology on six fronts, sometimes separate, sometimes overlapping.

Transition

Emphasis is not the only determinant for a particular organizational plan. In dealing with the specialized subject matter of business, the subject matter, or the writer's assigned relation to it, or the arrangement of the industry or company itself may dictate the natural and inevitable approach. Not only do considerations of emphasis exercise control, but the natural transitions between parts of the project also become influential. In bringing to light the inherent relationship of facts, the writer has a responsibility to do more than make mechanical connections.

"Mere arrangement," Coleridge held, "is not method." The writer has to see and to suggest possible connections. Overelaborating your transitions is as ineffective as overlooking them. The connection between separate parts should be left implicit if self-evident. At other times the reader needs an explicit direction as to where he is going next.

After a new heading, the first sentence may reidentify the full scope of material to be covered in that section. In doing so, the first sentence (or it may the first paragraph) will serve as an umbrella over the entire section. The lack of such a control device becomes apparent in the illustration that follows:

> *Mechanics*
>
> There is no excuse for me to misspell words . . .
>
> Early papers in the course contained glaring mistakes in grammar . . .

The student, in reporting on his written work, needed to signal his reader that he was discussing individual aspects of *Mechanics* as a whole. Transition breaks down without such a unifying device.

Inference and Fact

Inferences as well as facts are the responsibility of any thinking person. The significance of facts may lie chiefly in their inferential aspect. But there is a point to recognize here. As the thoughtful, constructive, creative report writer crosses the border from fact to inference, he must let his reader realize that there is a difference.

The following sentence from a salesman's proposal that an automobile manufacturer plan for more follow-up between the company and its dealers offers inference as well as fact:

> Personal contact will initiate a chain of events that will allow the well-specified objectives to be met and, being met, to increase the sale of cars.

"Personal contact," "chain of events," "specified objectives," "sale of cars," may reasonably be regarded as facts. In addition, a certain result is implied by the writer from the fact: "to increase." Here, however, the reader is not in danger of being hoodwinked. The phrase, "and, being met," constitutes a kind of pointer or indicator that the reader is being led to make an inference.

In your own writing, even before reaching the point where you are making an implication, you yourself, as the writer, must be clear as to the distinction. To lead your reader to draw an inference is not a mistake; in fact, it may be essential, as it was to the salesman quoted. But to permit an inference to be confused with a fact raises an ethical question. If the reader is not alerted as to what must be regarded as fact and what as inference, an inaccurate impression may result.

A report which has been presented consistently in factual language may suddenly introduce an implication which the reader swallows as fact without ever knowing it, as in this sentence from a designer of accounting systems:

> Your company is considering its internal audit system. To make the improvements desired, changes to emphasize cost accounting as required by the accounting authorities today are necessary immediately.

The inference comes from the inserted phrase, "as required by the accounting authorities today," of course.

Hersey, in *Hiroshima,* holds himself for the most part to objective, factual language. He declines, actually, to push his readers into specific inferences about atomic bombardment. So overwhelming are the possibilities in such a factual situation as the one described that he wants his readers to do their own inferring without suggestion from him. The facts are left to speak for themselves.

Distribution

The disposition of factual and inferential matter must accord with an over-all plan. Good organization finds and uses the preexisting links in the material, whatever its nature. Apart from the beginning and the end, the middle of a piece of work is important. Here it is, indeed, that the validity and the vitality of whatever precedes and follows are determined.

Of course, before you can test the interconnections of the parts of your report with the whole, you will set up, hypothetically and then finally, your sections. There must be some commensurability in their length and detail. From the divisions must come the balance you are seeking. From your distribution will be derived the sense of proportion in your presentation. Divide your material in order to rule it. Bacon, in his essay, "Of Dispatch," used words which we can apply to writing:

> Above all things, order, and distribution, and singling out of parts, is the life of dispatch; so as the distribution be not too subtle: for he that doth not divide will never enter well into business; and he that divideth too much will never come out of it clearly.

Hersey, in his meticulously organized report on the devastation of a city, demonstrates distribution. Most writers depend on obvious links to make the parts fit the whole. Hersey does so by what appears to be violation of transition. A passage about one of the victims, Father Kleinsorge, stops abruptly, saying his wounds "had suddenly opened wider. . . ." Then without explanation, the author takes up the case of Mrs. Nakamura, who had suffered no cuts or burns but whose hair now suddenly came out in combfuls. It might seem as if the continuity has been broken, but the contrary proves true. As Hersey's chronology moves forward, the first insignificant effects of the radiation are followed by more violent onsets in victim after victim. The connection lies in the context, inexorably so, but it is never pounded into the reader.

The word "method," Coleridge pointed out, "signifies a way of transit." Sometimes your own experience in working your way through your data will reveal the right route. But in getting your reader to follow you, you may have to turn the sequence around. Here, your chief help will come from thinking about your reader. Begin where he will begin. Work your way into the subject through what is familiar, or what is acceptable, or what is arresting to him. His point of view is worth respecting in your plan of presentation as well as in your wording. A report on initial exploration of outer space given to school children might have to begin differently from one made to a government authority.

If your thesis or proposal is likely to be resisted by your reader, you may be able to anticipate the counterarguments. If so, bring them forth and give your own answer, point by point. You may be able to take the wind out of your opponent's sails.

Point of View

The writer's own point of view, if clearly established at the outset and consistently expressed, will be something the reader can follow throughout the organized whole. Point of view in this sense means the literal use of that phrase—perspective rather than opinion. The reader needs to know enough about who is speaking to know whether to rely upon him, whether to take the writer's word in the matter or not. This is where the anonymous letter-writer limits his effect. The point of view behind the communication cannot be weighed when the source is unknown. Veracity, disinterestedness, authority, experience, judgment, taste, all enter into the credibility an author establishes through making his point of view clear.

One illustration of point of view is the use of the editorial "we." Newspapers observe the tradition in their editorial columns of pluralizing any use of the first-person pronoun in order to make the opinion expressed a joint one, as from the staff as a whole. An editorial is not meant to convey the outlook of one particular individual. Business reports often follow the same device. The name of the firm rather than of an individual may be appended. Hersey, scrupulous to give an objective account of the bombing, uses parentheses to signal his readers when he is speaking in the light of special knowledge instead of adhering to the point of view of the six people whose experiences he is recording:

> As they started up a valley away from the tight-ranked houses, the all-clear sounded. (The Japanese radar operators, detecting only three planes, supposed that they comprised a reconnaissance.)

The parentheses show us that Hersey is intentionally shifting the point of view.

In controlling the tone of a communication which you present from your own point of view in the first person, the pronoun "I" needs watching. Frequency produces an unfortunate tone. When repeated too often and when given the emphatic opening spot in a sentence, "I" sticks out like a sore thumb. The remedies are at your command. Eliminate some of the pronouns by use of the passive voice; play down others by moving them away from the beginning of a sentence or paragraph. Circumstances permitting, use of the first person singular is a natural, direct way of writing, however.

Another illustration of point of view not in business is that used in Victorian novels, when an author addressed himself directly to "Dear Reader." The use of "you," either outright or understood as in the imperative mood, is increasing in business and indicates that the writer is directly addressing his reader. "You" needs to be introduced, if it is going to be used, near the outset to fix the point of view, and then repeated often enough to keep the reader in the close touch that has been established.

One way to confuse and impede a reader is to switch the point of view without giving explicit notice that this is being done. Unannounced switching is an easy mistake to commit: "Faulty sentences are my greatest weakness," wrote one individual in evaluating his communications. "This is illustrated," he continued, "in the boss's comments on my reports and cumbersome reading of material written." The writer shifts in the last sentence from what the boss says to what he himself (as the writer) gets out of reading. Here is another sample: "The payroll checks are sent to the controller's office instead of sending them to the department supervisor." When the verb (send) is used first in the passive and then in the active voice, the subject changes, and with it the point of view from which the author is writing. Another example comes from an automotive engineer: "If failure does occur in the field, a two-part epoxy kit has been developed to glue the mirror bracket on."

Method Summarized

The considerations that enter into organizing a piece of written work are manifold: the nature of the material, the kind of reader, the decisions regarding emphasis, transition, the interplay of fact and inference, the distribution of parts, the point of view. There is no one right method of organization; however, within a given situation, there is a fitting, clarifying scheme of organization. To say that first things should come first may sound like a truism, but it may be as helpful a definition of good organization as there is. The writer, of course, is left with the fundamental decision as to what things are the first things. Organization that puts first those things that reasonably seem to belong there and puts what should be second, third, and so on in that sequence is fitting and illuminating.

For an instinctive sense of organization, it would be hard to find a stronger example than the composition written by a third-grader:

I Was a Boy Astronaut

> One day the President sent me a letter. It said, "Come to Cape Canaveral." I started to the airport. I got to Cape Canaveral by three planes.
>
> The President was by a big rocket ship.
>
> He said, "You must fly to the moon."
>
> I said, "At my age? I am only 8 years old."
>
> The President said, "Good. We need someone at your age."
>
> After I called my mother, she said, "Anything for the President."
>
> So three days later I got into my spaceship. I was sent to the moon. I set down my spaceship. I saw a moon man.
>
> I liked him and he liked me.
>
> We went back to earth. I was the world's best boy.

The report of the young astronaut (who was pointing himself *ad astra* early) was organized on a two-way pattern consisting of motion through space and motion through time. Not only does he adhere to his organizational scheme meticulously, but he achieves maximum credibility for the incredible. His achievement in the latter respect is by the same means used by Daniel Defoe in his hypothetical but amazingly credible *Journal of the Plague Year*. The way such authors make even the unbelievable believable is by reporting of exact detail. For what other reason should the aspiring young spaceman tell us he took three planes en route to Cape Canaveral? Not only that, but he neatly eliminated the skeptic's doubt over the matter of his age. To top off the whole timely, realistic, substantiated report, the author then presents his conclusion, wisely enough, in inductive fashion.

The arrangement of a classic like Washington Irving's "Rip Van Winkle" accounts for its unforgettableness. Purportedly a chronological report and not a story, this piece of writing enables us to peel off the layers in its presentation like an onion's skin, so perfectly does one seem to grow over another. Or you can analyze Poe's stories. In "A Cask of Amontillado," the pattern becomes that of a walk through a wine cellar, the pace intensifying till the dead end is reached. In Poe's "Descent into the Maelstrom," the sequence of events is that of the sudden squall preceded and followed by a calm, but with what a difference. In business reports, as in such narratives, the content must be made to march along a definite route.

Particularly in reports written to convey facts and ideas which the reader needs to remember, the organizational plan must make maximum use of the introductory and end sections. Repetition of content, though not of wording, may be built into these strategic spots like structural reinforcement. One unlettered but not unwise and surely helpful individual took it upon himself to write the city treasurer of St. Joseph, Missouri, as follows (the city treasurer's office decided thereupon to cease mailing out a certain tax delinquency statement): "For three years you have been told she don't live here. She don't live here. Lady is dead."

Most reports certainly contain three major segments. Bacon put it this way in describing the general process: "There be three parts of business: the preparation, the debate or examination, and the perfection." But the writer's task is also to point out any logical divisions within this triple-tiered structure of beginning, middle, and end. Having divided the material into comprehensible sections, the writer is no less obligated to point out the connections, the internal relationships, so that in the end he can add it all up for his reader. The result is organization or what Coleridge called "method." It is not an end in itself, but it is one of the means whereby a writer achieves his end.

Philip Sporn of the American Electric Power Company had in mind from his early foundry days the value of organization when he said:

> Writing is a mold poured around the ideas in the mind of the writer. No successful writing can be called that unless what comes out of the mold fits exactly the ideas originally entertained by the writer.

6: Facing the Circumstances

As you gain headway in doing a report, a memo, or a letter, you may look back over your tracks to see how you have got where you are. You have a road map in the outline you follow and can visualize the format your results will take. The means of locomotion you use are words, sentences, paragraphs. How fast you travel depends on these means. But before starting, the mission itself must be analyzed as to its reason and purpose.

Means and Ends of Communication

Almost every writer at some point wonders whether what he is doing is necessary, and if so whether he is going about it properly. You will be wise to face this question. At the source of a communication may lie the answer.

What gave rise to your project? Why was a report called for in the first place? Should the matter be handled otherwise? Perhaps a face-to-face conversation, if not a telephone call, would be better. Ways of communicating are multiplying.

One way to answer that general question was proposed several centuries ago by Bacon:

> It is generally better to deal by speech than by letter; and by the mediation of a third than by a man's self. Letters are good, when a man would draw an answer by letter back again; or when it may serve for a man's justification afterwards to produce his own letter; or where it may be danger to be interrupted, or heard by pieces. To deal in person is good, when a man's face breedeth regard, as commonly with inferiors; or in uncertain cases, where a man's eye upon the countenance

> of him with whom he speaketh may give him a direction how far to go; and generally, where a man will reserve to himself liberty either to disavow or to expound.

Since the days of that pragmatic man of affairs, the means available for conveying one's purposes have expanded. Few, however, have discriminated so nicely as did that Elizabethan financier in choosing the means to say what needs to be said:

> Reading maketh a full man; conference a ready man; and writing an exact man. . . .

The very ease and rapidity of communicating often results in unprofitable use of the process.

A Detroit executive, en route in his car to his office, enters into conversation with a counterpart in Tokyo. In not much more time, multiple copies of a memo roll out of a duplicating machine, relaying the decision they reached. The means are undeniably there. But what of the use being made of the means?

Among thoughtful businessmen, the alternatives available for conveying facts and ideas are being recognized. The use of the written word (and handwritten at that) remained paramount in business through the last century. How would Thomas Edison's dictum on the cost of current, sent longhand to "Friend Marks," be transmitted now? Would he telephone or dictate a letter or send a teletype message perhaps? Would he get different results?

Edison himself laboriously penned his important statement regarding the management of business affairs. No secretary refined such details as spelling. In our century, use of the penned or typed word faces competition. Businessmen are well aware of this. The live voice and the automated signal have become strong contenders with the piece of paper. Imaginative use of the communication process is an index to corporate viability. If yesterday's way of transmitting information, clarifying purposes, and enunciating policies is not today's, today's will scarcely be tomorrow's.

As a business grows in sales, payrolls, customers, suppliers,

Ogden Mine N.J.

April 7/91

Friend Marks

To my mind the raising of the price from 3/4 to 1 c per

lamp hour is a bid for competition. I am a beleiver

in Insuring the permanancy of an investment by

keeping prices so low that there is no inducement to

others to come in an ruin it,

There seems to be a law in commercial things as in

nature,

If one attempts to obtain more profit than general average

he is immediately punished by competitions.

Yours

Edison

Courtesy of The Henry Ford Museum, Dearborn, Michigan.

stockholders, capital, plants, products, and inventories, its need for communication intensifies. Achieving growth depends to a large extent upon successful communication. What are the possibilities open to the businessman for saying what he has to say?

To Write or Not to Write

The communicator decides whether to pick up the phone, to turn on the dictaphone, to program a computer, to draw a diagram, to call a conference, or just to pat someone on the back. As times change, new techniques are developed. Who would have thought, only yesterday, of telstar? Not so many generations ago, the crystal set was the miracle.

Not all methods are modern in origin. Reputedly, the whistle was relied upon during the fifteenth century on the rocky and hilly island of Gomera in the Canaries. Because of the terrain, a whistle would carry where the voice would not, and gossip, news, and messages could be exchanged. This "language," it is said, can still be heard among the residents of Gomera.

Smoke signals illustrate a nonverbal system, outmoded by the changes in American life. One ad man, seeking a promotion theme, visited an Indian reservation in the Southwest. After waiting in vain to see smoke signals, he finally asked one of the residents: "What *do* you do when you want to send messages to the next mesa?"

"Same as you," the Indian replied. "Telephone." What worked once is not always what works now.

The human word has shown its staying power, as has the human gesture. What has proved more expressive in our century than Churchill's upraised fingers in the sign of a V? Involved in this bit of eloquence are the Morse code, a Beethoven symphony, and a brave man's gesture. We need the full range of communication methods today.

Businessmen of the twentieth century face an information explosion. "Today only a fraction of new knowledge is being effectively recorded, analyzed, and communicated," declared Thomas J. Watson, Jr., President of International Business Machines Corporation. Can the transmission process keep pace with the acquisition of knowledge? The English language, though one of our strongest instrumentalities, is undergoing strain. Each discovery in science produces its own vocabulary. Each invention sets in motion the need for explanation. Specifically, each new piece of machinery installed in a plant has to be accompanied by procedural instructions of immediate intelligibility.

What is written on the job must be read, referred to, and remembered, or we have a product not worth the postage stamp to carry it or the space to file it. Though people need to know more, they want to read less. As the dimension of space expands, the dimension of time seems to contract; and reading takes time. In the explosion of matters to be communicated, the written word is meeting powerful competitors: the picture in mass media, the television program, the radio broadcast, even the subliminal possibility. Computers have more and more to contribute in data processing.

Is the written word, then, in a given situation, best? The answer to this honest query lies in recognizing the purpose of the communication: who is saying what to whom and why? The word, whether written or spoken, has never been more than one-of-many means of communicating. Nowadays, with transmission facilities ready and waiting to relay millions of words to millions of people, the word is the means most often employed. But different times and different places made the word less useful. Time and place and circumstance influence the means chosen for communicating.

The human means of communicating, whether written or spoken, have always had certain advantages as compared to mechanical means. Words are flexible; they are capable of instant adaptation to the user's needs. Words put on paper, as once on stone or parchment, outlive spoken words. The Rosetta stone holds the key to history.

When it comes to short-range history, businessmen nowadays find the written word indispensable for making their plans and transactions a matter of record. "Give me a memo" is a familiar comment, though one to be uttered with due deliberation. Memo writing may be resorted to as a cure-all for confusion and indecision at the source of a problem. As a substitute for listening and responding, it is extravagant. The investment in the high-priced time of dictator, transcriber, and reader bulks large in the cost picture. No less frequent than memos are the messages that orbit the world under postage stamps. Paper, properly put to work in reaching a solution, can lead to clarification, decision and action. And where would business be without reports substantiating proposals, spelling out reasons, citing evidence, convincing critics?

Watchfulness is required for every syllable, lest obscurity and inaccuracy result. It is possible that there are some individuals capable of clear thinking who are incapable of clear writing; but it is impossible for individuals to be capable of clear writing who are incapable of clear thinking. If ambiguities beset the spoken word, the reduction of a message to paper permits checking, revising—all the safeguarding of second thoughts.

The act of writing may prevent the inadvertent implications that are frequent in speaking. At a parochial school a priest was passing out report cards. Handing one to a first-grader, he said: "Son, you better try to get that 'D' off your card."

"Yes, Father," the boy replied. A few minutes later he was observed by his teacher busily erasing the mark. A casual word had been used to mean one thing by the well-intentioned Father but it had been taken to mean something quite different by the equally well-intentioned schoolboy. Who was responsible for this failure of communication? The communicator obviously miscalculated the response to his remark.

If such misadventures occur through conversation, care to avoid similar mistakes can be taken in the preparation of written messages. The truly professional person—the businessman, lawyer, doctor, or teacher no less than the full-time author—evinces his respect for the medium in which he is working, the language. Such a respect breeds care and attention to the fine points of clarity and conciseness. How else except by observing structural discipline in the style could such unfortunate double-meanings as these have been avoided:

> Salaries and wages can be determined from current payroll records. To these will be added the estimated department head bonuses . . .
>
> (ambiguity caused by problem of antecedent of "these")
>
> Physical inventory adjustment in these herds actually amount to adjustment of the births previously reported, and are so recorded.
>
> (ambiguity caused by nonagreement in numbers between verb, "amount" and verb, "are," with subject, "adjustment")
>
> . . . differences are created by the necessity to incorporate Engineering Changes in an expedient manner during the period preceding and immediately after a new model production start.
>
> (ambiguity caused by misplacement of modifying phrase "during. . . .")

If the hazards of written English deter a businessman from using it, he is not playing on one whole octave of his keyboard in communication. It may seem easier to phone, or to surround one's self in a committee room, or even to make no response at all. A sense of insecurity about writing comes from unfamiliarity with its intricacies. But the choice as to means of communicating should be made for positive instead of negative reasons.

Writing is costly to writer and reader alike, but it is extravagant only when it does not succeed. The written word may fail because of its own length and complexity. The written word may misfire if sent to the wrong individual at the wrong time. The rightly chosen word, dispatched at the strategic moment, often travels farther and lasts longer than its competitors in the communication process. Much of the criticism of memo-itis is caused not by writing but by *bad* writing.

A moratorium on reports was recently ordered by New York City's superintendent of public schools. "The number of unnecessary—and often unread—reports is beyond belief," he explained. The reasons for this reaction would be echoed in executive offices everywhere. Once a businessman brings forth a report—often a difficult and unwelcome assignment—the natural step is to set the duplicating machines whirring. Multiple copies emerge in no time. They are sped up, down, and across, coming to rest in already crowded in-baskets. Are they read? Or is there a quick trip from the cradle to the grave of the filing cabinet?

Actual consumption of written matter is hard to measure in business but an informed guess would place it below the level of expectations. If the value from intake is not commensurate with the effort of output, the reason may be two-fold: quantity and quality. The quantity of paperwork is attributable in part to a desire for security.

In the barrage of daily transactions, in the rapid-fire of decisions, the temptation is to take refuge behind a barricade of records. Once a memo has been requested, its *raison d'être* can, for the moment anyway, be dismissed. The executive mind is absolved of responsibility. Making everything a matter of record is itself no solution.

Overreliance on written communications defeats the essential purpose of this method of conveying information and ideas. Gresham's Law can be applied to more than money matters: bad writing will drive out the good. Too many words, poorly prepared, will kill the potential value of well-drafted, well-aimed letters, memos, and reports.

Businesses are constantly reviewing and testing their internal and external communications. In offices all over the country, the question comes up daily: to write or not to write? The total spectrum of communication provides different ways of getting a point over to a colleague, a customer, a client, or an employee. Selection of the best way can be made from a wide range of alternatives, from simple gesture to teletype, from a handwritten note to a documented survey. If the decision is to put the matter on paper, the dividends of precision and permanence should accrue.

Prior Considerations

Writing exacts logical thought processes, pins the writer down. It provides a record. It gives readers a tangible basis of judgment, a platform for action. It can be made an instrument of influence, persuasion, belief. It can be directed to a selected readership: the one, the few, or the many. The word itself may be supplemented with graphic illustrations, oftentimes in color. A whole chain of decisions is linked with the decision to put a matter in writing. As a purveyor of facts and ideas, writing remains the most reliable means.

Foreseeing Implications

To whom should the word be addressed? And by whom? What should be the form, the structure, the tone, the style? For example, the man in the gray flannel suit decided not to communicate certain information in a certain situation, not to tell what he considered the most significant fact about himself in applying for a job. Once it has been decided to handle a problem in writing, however, you need to foresee advantages and possible disadvantages in committing the situation to paper.

Relating Sender and Receiver

Before the structural reinforcement of the Electra plane, a series of crashes shook public confidence in this aircraft. One of the airlines using it—American—took stock of the unfavorable publicity at a staff conference concerning the overall Electra problem. How could the public be convinced of the safety precautions? top management asked itself. The problem was to put across "the true facts about the Electra," one senior officer commented.

At the initiative of the executive officers of the airline, the decision was to make a two-fold presentation in writing. The president personally wrote and signed a letter reaffirming the American Airlines' operating philosophy and sense of responsibility for the passengers:

> If we believed the Electra to be unsafe, we would ground it. . . . But, on the basis of all the facts available to us, there is no good reason why the Electra should be grounded.

This strongly worded reassurance was addressed to the group of influential friends and customers known as the "Admirals." With the president's letter was enclosed another, signed by one of the company's engineering test pilots. He gave technical details in evidence of the Electra's safety, "a pilot's airplane" as he called it. The double communication received national attention through the press.

Behind the joint approach lay the desire to convince the readers that an individual of special competence and expertness was willing to give his word as to the Electra's safety. The president's letter was, of course, subject to the skeptic's reaction: "Oh, him? He has his career, not his life, at stake. Of course, he's got to say the plane is OK." Not so the pilot, who in his letter was staking his life upon his willingness to fly the Electra. Credibility was related to the writer's point of view. The importance of who it is that writes is often as great as what is written. In the particular instance, the directing of the missives to the Admirals reflected the importance of still another consideration, the matter of whom the letters were addressed to.

Did the communication process as employed in this situation prove helpful? The signatures, the recipients, and the form of the letters were all studiously planned, just as the content was carefully organized and composed. "Yes, we feel these letters have served the purpose for which they were written," the vice-president and general manager confirmed some weeks later. The question as to effectiveness was also put to a class of students studying communication in business. Only one contrary possibility was noted. Though Electras had suffered accidents on other lines besides American, the plane may have become identified in the minds of some with that one airline, accidents and all, as a result of the letter campaign.

Saving Time

In considering what and how you write, consider the circumstances in which your communication will be read, the receptivity or lack of it at the other end. Will it be read amid noise and interruptions at an office? Will your reader be rushed? The answer is probably "Yes." Lest we think our age is the only one short of time, we might recall Bacon's maxim:

> For time is the measure of business, as money is of wares; and business is bought at a dear hand where there is small dispatch.

Decreasing the amount of written matter is one way to increase its palatability. Use of the toll call, telegram, and teletype are frequent alternatives or supplements. It is sometimes less easy to catch another person's eye than ear. But when things are put in writing, conciseness helps. The modern executive will cast his eye over a one-page document when he instinctively puts aside longer documents for a later perusal (which may never come).

Use of a regular format sometimes accelerates its comprehensibility. Many companies have standardized their report forms for this reason. Staff members know ahead of time where to look for what they want to find. The writer has to walk a tightrope between familiarity and boredom, between innovation and confusion. The use of the familiar pattern will often save not only the reader's time but the writer's too. The element of variety can be incorporated into other aspects such as style. Use of a familiar form is an automatic means to establish contact.

Speed in communicating comes from working on a deadline. A deadline cuts down the time for writing and thereby acts as some control on the amount. Space can advantageously be kept within bounds by the number of words to be used. Compressing is almost always possible with a blue pencil. "It is sheer laziness," protested Churchill, "not compressing thought into reasonable space." Devices like parallel construction and tabulation save space. Adjectival and adverbial modifiers may be sacrificed. Repetition can be pared to the essential minimum. Not only can documents be kept short but they can also have the appearance, the look, of brevity. It may take more time to write a short communication, however, than a long one. Length relates to ease of reading as well as the number of pages. Contractions like "I'll" and "they'd" and "won't," suitable for informal presentations, are useful in speeding a reader over a line. Nothing, of course, lengthens a handwritten message more than illegibility.

Communicating Unmistakably

No matter how concisely you may write, it does not help if you do not say what you mean to say. On the assumption that your facts and the inferences to be drawn therefrom are correct, the matter of imparting them accurately is at stake. Very often communication breaks down at this phase. A patient, given a new prescription, assumed that he would have no difficulty carrying out his doctor's orders. What he read, however, on the label of the medicine bottle was this: "Take one pill before each meal with at least one glass of water." (How many glasses of water in a day? In fact, how many meals?)

Some time ago, in a magazine a cartoon appeared showing two little urchins passing each other in opposite directions along the street. "Where ya going?" asks one.

"I ain't a'goin. I'm a'comin," replies his pal with indignation. It's all in a word; if not all, a great deal. To convey the simplest message precisely is far from easy, words and groups of words being as transmutable as they are.

During wartime in a small Connecticut town, many poignant farewells were witnessed at the local railroad station. One day, a young mother whom the stationmaster had previously seen saying goodby to her soldier husband returned to the platform, her small son held tightly by the hand. "What time," she inquired, "does the next train go through?"

"Which way? New York or Boston?" the stationmaster wanted to know.

"It doesn't matter," she replied, eyeing the tracks. Not

until the New York-bound express roared through and the young woman had a chance to show her little boy the "chu-chu" did the stationmaster dare leave her side.

The words in themselves are not entirely responsible for the way a reader interprets them. It is the words in relation to the situation that can cause trouble. In a totally new situation, where there is little or no common knowledge between "sender" and "receiver," problems may occur. The oral facility exhibited by the astronauts and their ground personnel was strikingly matched by their lucidity, selectivity, and colloquialism. The success of the space flights depended in part upon the precision, accuracy, and conciseness of their two-way conversation. The lack of precedent for the experience, the unfamiliarity of the situation, was the chief difficulty the astronauts had to overcome in conveying essential data and reactions. Normally, people depend on context as well as words to express themselves. Context (i.e., situation) was nonexistent in the earliest flights into outer space.

The first astronauts used "we" in reporting their experiences even while in orbit, where they most certainly were alone. Some commentators implied that the first astronaut used the plural pronoun in this situation to refer to himself and the Deity. Others took the use of "we" to mean that the astronaut was speaking for all his supporting personnel as well as for himself. No man likes to be alone with the unknown. When the later astronauts reported their experiences, the "we" disappeared and "I" was used. The element of newness was wearing off. No longer did the spacemen feel they were venturing into the unknown and, for that reason, they may have felt less in need of conjointness.

The situational hazards in written communications can be reduced by anticipation of the reader's state of mind. Humor, when it succeeds, can bring you into instantaneous contact, but when it fails you may never retrieve yourself. Imagination and sensitivity to the reader's state of mind are needed. An expression that, on the face of it, was very funny led a gas company customer to a dead-end as far as further response to her complaint was concerned. She reported what appeared to be a mistake in her bill, computed by electronic data processing. When the clerk, on the telephone, stated that the computer had not erred, the customer wrote a letter to the company saying: "If you cannot get through to your machines, take me to your leader." The "leader" letter was filed away, without action by the one who opened it, without being shown to the manager. The humor did not seem funny to its immediate reader. When the customer got no answer, she wrote the local newspaper. The matter developed into a public attack upon the company with further letters to the editor and to the state's public utility commission.

Who will and who won't see what you write? Is it or is it not confidential? One way to place yourself in step with your intended reader is to stop and think of him, to visualize him, before you start to write him. Go further, if the subject is complex or touchy: role-play his reactions to what he is going to be hearing from you. By putting yourself in his shoes, by sitting in his desk chair, you will gain insight. You will intuitively shape your communication to meet the situation.

Factually, you may take too much previous knowledge of a subject for granted so that the reader is soon lost. Or you may insult or bore him by not taking enough for granted. Does he want to follow your reasoning or will he be inclined to disagree? You have to be imaginative about the human side of your reader. Guard against the cliché, "As you know. . . ."

We all know what was meant by the first person who said he wished he had bitten off his tongue. Regret for mistaken, misguided, misdirected, or misquoted communication is often painful, particularly if it has been put in writing. Sometimes, overcommunication may prove to be its own downfall as the media and means multiply. Perhaps the late Dame Edith Sitwell, the English poet and personality, had some such notion in mind when, in *Who's Who,* she listed her hobby as "Silence."

Avoidance of putting certain matters in writing is not uncommon. In 1963 the directors of the Franklin National

Bank in New York agreed to discontinue smoking at directors' meetings and committee sessions. This policy was subsequently communicated to the bank's officers at their regular meeting. The officers were asked to inform the employees at their regular meeting that they would have to use the washrooms if they wished to smoke during working hours. No signs were posted and no memos were circulated. The matter became an issue at the annual stockholders' meeting and was publicized throughout the country.

Clarifying Motives

In an embarrassing episode of misunderstanding at a high level of political and business life, both the written and the spoken word were responsible. In 1961 a petroleum company's representative in Washington sent a letter to several dozen other gas and oil representatives saying: "Secretary Udall [Stewart L. Udall, Secretary of the Interior], who happens to be a friend of long standing, has asked me as a personal favor to him to solicit the oil and gas industry in Washington in an effort to help the Secretary dispose of his 'very sizeable' quota of tickets for the Jefferson-Jackson Day Dinner."

After Secretary Udall received from the author a copy of the letter, which had also been quoted in the press, he telephoned asking the author to try to recall it. When criticisms from his political opponents were printed, he released a statement explaining that he was "appalled" and "flabbergasted"; that the letter writer had gone "far beyond what I had intended when I said that I hoped he and his friends would attend the dinner." But this did not forestall more newspaper stories, and the Secretary subsequently said: "I should have written all of them a letter [he was referring to the fifty-six recipients] disavowing his letter immediately." And the author himself, before the date of the Jefferson-Jackson Day Dinner, issued a statement with the permission of his company: "Had it ever occurred to me that my motives might be misinterpreted, it is obvious that I would never have written any letters."

At least two failures to convey what was intended can be

pin-pointed: misunderstanding of an oral communication (Udall to company representative) and misunderstanding of a written communication (letter writer to the fifty-six addressees). The blunder might have been prevented by:

Realization of the proposition's implication
Careful choice between the oral and the written word
Precise and explicit selection of words
Forethought as to the total audience likely to hear of the message.

The proposition was: attendance at a political dinner. In any such communication the determining factors might have been isolated by considering who was saying what, and why, to whom, and how?

Considering the Reader

Giving sufficient consideration to the reader is hard for subject-oriented writers. Professional people become buried in their own data. Vice-President Theodore O. Yntema of Ford stressed as one of the first requisites to effective communication the need for "understanding of your audience." To communicate adequately, you must interpret. To interpret, you must understand the other fellow. Only by such understanding can you adapt your content, a most efficacious and yet simple process.

The possible ethical implications arising from adaptation are made transparent by a quotation taken from another era and another calling—Elizabethan statecraft:

> If you would work any man, you must either know his nature and fashions, and so lead him; or his ends, and so persuade him; or his weakness and disadvantages, and so awe him; or those that have interest in him, and so govern him.

The words are Bacon's and the subject, "Of Negotiating."

In adaptation the goal or purpose holds the secret of justifiability. Adaptation is a means to an end. Since it will be conducive to the achievement of one's objective, the only question is whether the objective is ethical. Writers must adapt but not alter their conclusions to suit their particular readers. Such a process springs from a sense of values.

Tone is the human factor involved here. You can readily connect what we are talking about with the phenomenon noted by Courtney C. Brown, Dean of the Columbia University School of Business: that is, "the progressive emergence of human factors in the operation of a business." Tone is the subtlest but not the most obvious quality in the written page. For it is not reducible to rules of grammar, principles of logic, or psychological calculation.

For contrast in tone, sales letters from British firms take a respectful, dignified attitude which sets them apart from the casual, hail-fellow-well-met approach of some American firms. On a letterhead displaying the coveted appointment to serve the monarch, Thomas Goode & Company (London) Ltd., commences:

> Dear Sir,
>
> Having been privileged to receive your esteemed patronage in the past, we feel you will be interested. . . .

The complimentary close is in keeping with the humble though not obsequious tone:

> We have the honor to be,
> Sir,
> Your obedient servants

Almost any American sales letter will illustrate a difference in tone. Here is how the New York Life Insurance Company starts a letter to a prospective customer (without any salutation):

> I am planning to stop in to say "hello" to you some day soon. . . .

and the communication ends simply:

> Sincerely yours,

Whatever the country of origin, a tone of warmth and sincerity, of dignity and naturalness, does wonders. Above all, the tone should sound like you or the organization you represent. The elusive yet important matter of tone was what Churchill was getting at with his Home Secretary: "Many thanks for showing me your notes for your speech on the colonial policy . . . ," he wrote in 1943. "I should have thought you could have a more confident ring."

The tone may change in writing as it changes in speaking when one turns from, say, a new employee to an old, or from a neighbor to a passerby. External factors such as the recipient, the time, and the place alter wording, sequence, even content. Internal factors such as the writer's self, his employment, his temperament and mind, his purposes, his tastes produce more subtle differences. Tone is not something that can be bought and applied like a poultice. It is not something synthetic but arises, when authentic, from the nature of the situation and the nature of the writer. "One can usually put one's thoughts better in one's own words," commented Churchill.

To do justice to the constant elements and the variable elements in an interchange requires that you adapt the written word. The tone of our times, in business, as reflected in its paper work, has been informal, personal, outgoing, promising, vigorous. What it will be by the end of the century is guesswork, but more dignity, directness, and simplicity may be likely guesses as to the trend business will show. Tone that is unduly provocative, overcasual, experimental, or calculating is likely to wear itself out. The tendency to use "baby talk," to underestimate the public's level, will be defeated by the growth in higher education, in travel, in the standard of living.

Using Channels

Writing of the kind that we have been discussing is directed to some person or persons for some purpose or purposes. Lack of adaptation is lack of one dimension in such communication. The total environment of the writer enters into his efforts. Pressures in the environment of business in the twentieth century require a writer on the job to be concise but complete, authoritative but tactful, sensitive to the reader but definite in his own mind. The writer must give conscious consideration, in advance, to the basic factors underlying the use of the communication process.

Who is it that is going to write something to *whom? How* can it best be done? *Where* and *when?* To these questions might be prefixed the even more essential one of whether to do it at all, and the answer to this question arises from the most primary query of all: *Why?* The problem of problems in business communication is not grammar; it is not form. It is situational blindness.

Business situations themselves hold the answers on when and how to communicate. One executive, Robert P. Briggs, Executive Vice-President of Consumers Power Company of Michigan, urges expanded use of the written word on the job and in the community and nation. "It is the responsibility of every business and business leader to weigh communications well and to exercise real leadership through meaningful communication." His plea, "Let's start talking, writing, and communicating," was predicated upon another plea: "Let's put our convictions into understandable language."

7: Putting Language To Work

If you turn out a methodically organized memo in accordance with all specifications, it still may not suffice. If you follow proper form, you will not necessarily succeed. Not even knowing what the situation calls for by way of a communication is enough. Your draft must also avoid certain prevailing hazards and conform to expected practices concerning the units of our language: the word, the sentence, and the paragraph.

These expected practices constitute a kind of linguistic arithmetic, an addition, subtraction, and multiplication performed with the letters of the alphabet. Here are the beginnings of style, what you might call the start of your own policy, your own feeling about what is most valid for the expression of the facts and ideas in your mind.

With a policy worked out for individual use of language, the writer must go on to the mathematics of it, and then to higher mathematics. The possibilities of language, for those who work with its integers systematically, unfold through a lifetime. Actually, a policy in something like style is seldom perfected, not even in the lifetime of a Chaucer, a Bacon, a Churchill. Far more is involved than meets the reader's eye:

> Language is the armory of the human mind; and at once contains the trophies of its past, and the weapons of its future conquests.

These words were uttered in the nineteenth century by Samuel Taylor Coleridge but, significantly, were quoted in the twentieth century by the Container Corporation of America in a nationwide advertisement.

One way of developing a functional style for everyday use is to recognize some of the symptoms that afflict writing in business today. They are as characteristic of us as the stylistic extremes of the Victorians were characteristic of them a century ago.

Seven Symptoms of Unworkable Language

The disorder prevalent in contemporary communication itself is well recognized. Dwight D. Eisenhower, when President, spoke of "the sea of semantic disorder" around us "in which old labels no longer faithfully describe." George Orwell, in his essay, *Politics and the English Language,* inveighs against "bad habits" of modern English, "especially written English," which are "spread by imitation." Protests about the abuse of language in the field of business abound: "By all odds, the most conspicuous deficiency in the college graduates we hire," declared General Electric's Manager of Marketing Personnel Development Service, "is their inability to communicate."

Though the reasons why words fail are as numerous and individual as the reasons why they succeed, some seven difficulties are symptomatic of the paper work of present-day business:

Indulging in figurative laxity
Universalizing
Making incompatible connections
Violating parallelism in structure and content
Escaping into pleasantries
Repeating disadvantageously
Pyramiding modifiers.

The seven symptoms are only a selection, but the selection is based on frequency and importance. These symptoms, taken together, add up to a disorder not of writing alone but of the thinking that forms and informs the writing.

The thinking phase contributes as much to style as the actual process of writing. Relationships between words, sentences, and paragraphs can be clarified and intensified by thinking through precisely what it is you want to say. What is troubling us, in other words, is nothing so superficially remediable as, for instance, lack of grammar, misspelling, monotony, or even length. The truth of it is that the quality of mind stands revealed by the quality of writing. As the thought goes, so goes the pen. An underlying difficulty can be traced to the writer's habits of mind and work. In his mind and work, consequently, lies the hope of treatment and cure.

Indulging in Figurative Laxity

Figures of speech, laboriously inculcated from our school days, do something that literal expressions cannot do, notably in poetry. In functional writing, the question is, do you want to do what the figure of speech can do? In business, communication must often be precise and definable.

When a businessman writes that his program is "off the ground" does he mean by this comparison from the field of aviation that his program is barely starting or that it is in full operation? The metaphor is open to more than one interpretation. As Charles L. Stevenson, the philosopher, has pointed out in his book, *Ethics and Language*:

> There is no such thing as giving an exact translation of a metaphor into nonmetaphorical terms. One can only give interpretations, and these are only approximate.

Figurative expressions not only subject the user to being misinterpreted but also to being meaningless. The reason for the meaninglessness of many figurative expressions is their overuse. Expressions like "get off the ground," "be in the swing," "like a shot," "nip in the bud," "as free as the air" have all been used so often that they cover a multitude of different ideas. Like worn-out elastic, they can take in a great many things without holding any of them (a simile itself).

The schoolboy's sin, the mixed metaphor, is another risk attendant upon indulgence in figurativeness. One engineer's report contained the following example: "If unpredicted events cause a pipe line to lag or stop, rapid repairs must be made." Even when read in context, the fairer test, it is impossible for you to visualize a pipe line "lagging." Here is another confused picture: "No one tool can sufficiently appraise every factor of company performance. A battery of tools is usually used." Tools do not "appraise" nor do they come in batteries. A personnel man, struggling with staff fluctuation, wrote that he would have to "iron out the peaks and valleys." For the image he created of a housewife trying to take her iron to the Blue Ridge Mountains, he got only laughter. To do its job, a figure of speech must present one consistent picture or image for the mind's eye. A mixed metaphor is like the photograph developed from a double exposure of the film.

A fresh, pertinent, unconfused figure of speech, unlike the overused, mixed, loose one, may affix your point more memorably, of course, than literal wording. Here is a current simile from a *Primer for Programming with the Mad Language*:

> Learning to write programs in the MAD language, i.e., learning to use the computer, is analogous to learning to drive the automobile. One may perfect the former technique without acquiring much knowledge of the computers themselves.

For businesslike communication, avoid lapsing unconsciously into figurative language. You may be taken as saying something other than what you mean or as saying nothing at all. The original, apt comparison or nonliteral word will do wonders, but it takes thinking, imagination, and care to conceive. The very currency of many figures of speech deprives them of the impact they once possessed.

Universalizing

An unnecessary risk was assumed by the report writer who said: "This new drug is in its infancy and like all available anticancer drugs it is capable of producing serious side effects." The risk is in the use of "all." The writer includes every single anticancer drug ever produced.

Universalizing is not only risky from the point of view of accuracy; it has, in communications which seek to be convincing, another drawback. When anyone makes a sweeping statement, sweeping to the extent of excluding so much as one doubtful statement, his reliability will be questioned. What happens when you read: "There was every indication that the Company does not know where it is going"? It is only human nature on the reader's part to think up the faintest possibility of contradicting exclusive assertions of the truth. A guarded statement is usually the more credible, human suspicion of human error being what it is. This is the reason for the old soap ad alleging "99-44/100%" purity. How much more believable this is than "100%."

Not only does a universalization, true or untrue, arouse the doubting Thomas in every reader. It often is actually untrue. A marketing specialist saw the trap into which he had fallen as soon as it was pointed out by his readers: "The primary object of any forecasting service is to maintain reasonable customer service." It is scarcely true that forecasting the weather has as its primary object reasonable customer service.

Making Incompatible Connections

So far, in both types of error discussed among writers in the business world, it is confusion of thought which has led to confusion of expression.

The same origin accounts for the "non sequitur" (it does not follow). Cause and effect relations are so important that the reader becomes aware quickly of any fallacy in tying them together, intentional or otherwise. "Because of the difficulty of establishing a person's capacity, it is impossible to grade everyone on an individual basis," wrote one school administrator. He knew, of course, that many reasons exist for not grading everyone on an individual basis. "Since the drug industry is aware," wrote the financial analyst, "of the consumer's rising discretionary income and the resulting possible increased demand, greater research to develop new products will be carried on." He did not, as it turned out, mean that research for new products would not be carried on anyway for reasons other than mercenary ones.

The illogical interrelating of ideas within sentences glares out at the reader after such a relationship is committed to paper. But the writer, putting his pen to that paper, may be blind and deaf to what he is saying. His words fail him. And the reason, often as not, comes from a desire to speed up his communication, to cover more ground in every sentence, to run together the thoughts that do have a relationship, though not the relationship conveyed by the words used.

Violating Parallelism in Structure and Content

Parallelism in language means saying similar things similarly. Parallelism is psychologically necessary where readers, wittingly or unwittingly, expect it. Readers become conditioned in matters of language usage; not only do they like to see certain things in certain places, but they have to see them as anticipated if they are to get the writer's meaning readily.

"A financial, product, and legal analysis will be made," declared one quality-control man in a manufacturing company. What did he mean? Was he going to analyze his company's product from the point of view of financial law? If so, the three words in his series are not equal in content as was the implication. The reader, seeing them written in positions of equality (i.e., in a series), is confused. Or did the expert mean that he was going to analyze the product of his company from its financial aspect, its qualitative aspect, its legal aspect? If so, the three words are not equal in structure as the writer intended and as the reader expects them to be.

The conditioning of human nature applies to reading as to other branches of human behavior. A reader is really trying to play the game of follow-the-leader (i.e., the writer). Communication, being a two-way process, is based on understood relationships between letters, syllables, words, phrases, sentences, paragraphs, chapters, volumes. That is why a writer, to save time, resorts to devices like the series. The series is meant to say the same thing about more than one thing simultaneously. Hence the implicit need for sameness in structure and content.

The series is only one of the spots where a reader expects parallelism. In headings, in tables of contents, in tabulations, for instance, the writer is trading on the understood sense of sameness. Parallelism carefully observed by the writer facilitates the reader in comprehending. When the reader sees the same elements in a sentence similarly placed he unconsciously expects that they will be similar in two respects: content and structure.

Items of disproportionate value as far as content is concerned should not be presented in similar structure, or the values will be confused—as here:

> Metal, wood, and transportation are necessary to industry.

Items of proportionate value, if presented in proportionate structure, seem proportionate. In a sentence describing the duties of a follow-up man, the author very properly made use of parallelism to name two alternatives available in a particular situation:

> When a vendor is behind schedule, it is the responsibility of the follow-up man to contact the vendor and get the material shipped or get a promise as to when it will be shipped.

When parallelism is violated by switches either in content or in structure, confusion is inevitable. Think of your reader as climbing a flight of stairs. He expects every step to be the same height. If one has a different rise to it from the rest, the climber will stumble.

Escaping into Pleasantries

The vogue of the pleasant and the positive, in sweeping American life, has swept business and the language of American business. The theory is that the more pleasant and positive the presentation of a subject, the more it appeals to a reader. Certainly, people read more readily what they like to read, just as they listen more willingly to what they enjoy hearing. Again, the thinking process is father to the writing process.

The lengths to which business, with its undeniable "selling" obligation, has gone to sound affirmative rather than negative are equaled in many other professional fields. A committee of junior high-school teachers in New York, appointed to find ways of saying things more tactfully on report cards, came up with such substitute suggestions as:

Lazy =Needs ample supervision in order to work well.

Selfish =Needs help in learning to enjoy sharing with others.

Truant =Needs to develop sense of responsibility in regard to attendance.

When what has to be communicated is not pleasant or positive, the question is how to get it read and accepted. Much stylistic effort has been directed to rendering the unpleasant pleasant by means of wording, to making the negative positive. The effort to be positive obviously is necessary for writers who tend to make negative statements in order to play it safe or to be cautious. For instance, a paragraph in one report began:

> We want to open a new plant near the home office. We can't do so until we have more capital. Furthermore, among the adjacent suburbs, all but two have prohibitive zoning restrictions.

This paragraph can be translated from the negative to the positive:

> We want to open a new plant near the home office. As soon as we have sufficient capital, we can proceed. In two adjacent suburbs, the zoning regulations would facilitate our plans.

The writer has retained his caution and accuracy but has shown what is possible rather than what is impossible.

The negative approach is less productive of concurrence and action than is the positive manner of writing. People give up when told "No" too often. Discouragement leads to inaction. Use of negative wording forces the reader to overcome barriers and takes him in, if at all, by the back door.

What writers on-the-job need to consider, in conjunction with thinking about the obvious benefit of positive presentation, is the build-up of reader resistance to any calculated approach, including the positive one. The letter that commences off the subject, for instance, with some innocuous pleasantry, today raises the recipient's suspicion of its real import; he skips to the midsection, anticipating that he will find the bad news buried there.

Business, which runs on foresight as much as hindsight, must become conscious of the public's growing sophistication. Underestimating people's psychological awareness has been prevalent in the standards of American communication. Readers with and without college degrees have caught on to the practice of being positive just for the sake of being so and now take offense.

What readers want is the flat-footed statement, even if it requires the use of a negative particle. What we think we want and what we can take and still come up smiling may be different, of course. So the wise, constructively minded writer is best advised to follow a genuine, natural approach. What is written without contrivance, without ulterior scheming, will scarcely end up with a negative impact provided the writer keeps in mind two things: the final objective (in itself, seldom negative) and the control of emphasis. The straightforward, time-saving statement is preferred by most readers to the elaborate euphemism, either of phrase or approach.

Repeating Disadvantageously

So simple and so obvious a fault is the recurrence of the same word or phrase or even point in subject matter that frequency of this fault is surprising. Other handicaps may be hard to eliminate, but you have only to reread your draft to be hit in the eye by unintentional repetition. The disadvantage is that the reader becomes bored. He says to himself that he doesn't need to be told the same thing twice.

Actually, we do need to be told some things not only twice but more than that in order to grasp them. Repetition, in a report, is obligatory as between the introduction and the summary, for example. Transition is based on repetition in the sense of carrying over a thought. But other words can be substituted, other phrases, other sentence structures, to say the same thing.

Intentional repetition can be of great advantage in style: "Dr. Sasaki . . . stopped working as a skillful surgeon," Hersey wrote in reporting on Hiroshima. ". . . he became an automaton, mechanically wiping, daubing, winding, wiping, daubing, winding." Business takes less spectacular advantage of the device of repetition, relying upon it less as a matter of wording than as a means of restating salient points. What most everyday writers need to do about repetition is to avoid doing it unintentionally, either as to style or content. The blue pencil is the right tool.

Pyramiding Modifiers

One generally undiagnosed condition is threatening writers in the world of business. In the effort to meet the demand for brevity, to save space, to cut everything possible, words used as modifiers are being piled on top of each other, pyramid fashion. The following sentence, written by a budget man in the automobile industry, offers the reader one difficulty apart from its length:

> *The index budget profit* shown in the *"Budget at Index Volume" column* should be adjusted by *the variable profit* applicable to *the total sales volume variance* from *the index budget,* using *the total divisional index budget variable profit rate.*

The subject words (substantives or nouns) with their attendant modifiers (traditionally adjectives) have been especially noted for our purposes. You will see not only the quantity of modifiers but something else about them. Only five of the seventeen modifying words are regular adjectives. Of the dozen others, many are themselves nouns.

The tendency to make nouns modify nouns can be characterized as pyramiding. True, it takes a little less space for the reader to see "the index budget profit" than to see "the profit in the index budget." However, it takes him more time to grasp because he is conditioned as all readers are to deriving some of the sense from stable grammatical structure. He may stop to supply the missing prepositional links himself. Overcompression of style necessitates a translating process in the reader's mind.

When you have recognized, as a reader, your dependence upon the stability of syntax, you can see why pyramiding of modifiers is confusing. One or two exceptions can be digested by the average reader, but what the writer began to do in moderation for space saving has become an epidemic:

> Routing instructions were not placed on accounts payable copies of orders.
>
> The machine printed parts index sheets to be used will reduce reading effort.
>
> The high leaf-tobacco inventory requirement produces complications.

Pyramiding makes its appearance first in the communications that circulate within a company, where the writer can trade upon the familiarity of his coworkers with his terminology:

> The approved injection molded rear quarter inside trim weld will also include the covering for the rear door pinch weld flanges to eliminate the separate pinch on the windlace assemblies.

What starts as private language soon makes its way into more general communications. Then the reader not only marks time but loses it. The turnover in business staffs and the continuous process of decentralization are cautions against dependence (even for internal messages) upon communications of restricted intelligibility.

The specific ailments noted as besetting the written communications of everyday affairs are only seven. The difficulties caused by the old pitfalls of uncoordinated paragraphs, winding sentences, imprecise words are now well known. The special difficulties caused in current business dealings by other pitfalls in language usage need recognition as well. The results are obvious: ambiguity, obscurity, sheer unintelligibility.

Summary of Suggestions

What can you decide upon as an advantageous policy in your use of the written language? Your decision will follow upon making certain other decisions:

> Does the situation require me to send something in writing, or does it require a conference, a call, an interview?
> Who will read what I write?
> What form of communication shall I use: letter, report, memo, news release?
> How shall I organize my subject?

With these questions answered, go on from there to adapt your writing to the project in hand. Adaptation is a large part of language usage.

If you are writing as a businessman to another businessman, it will be good policy to write in as short a space as the subject permits. But clarity is even more essential than brevity. Clarity is aided by concrete wording, simple sentences, easy transitions between unified paragraphs. Mark Twain, in a letter to a school boy, gave his prescription for writing:

> Dear Watt Bowser,
>
> Now I have read your composition, and think it is a very creditable performance. I notice that you use plain, simple language, short words, and brief sentences. That is the way to write English—it is the modern way, and the best way. Stick to it; don't let fluff and flowers and verbosity creep in. When you catch an adjective, kill it. No, I don't mean that utterly, but kill the most of them—then the rest will be valuable. They weaken when they are close together, they give strength when they are wide apart. An adjective-habit, or a wordy, diffuse, or flowery habit, once fastened upon a person, is as hard to get rid of as any other vice.
>
> Mark Twain

Wordiness and weakness take the interest out of reading. Today, interest is a factor of increasing importance because of the competition for the reader's time. Nothing so sensational as suspense or stylistic tricks may be necessary (alliteration or onomatopoeia, for example) ; but avoidance of repetition in wording, of monotony in sentence structure, of disorganization, and of grammatical violations is only sensible as the means to hold the reader's attention and respect.

Taking conspicuous liberties with grammatical tradition is offensive to many people. Readers incline to attribute minor infractions of the old rules to ignorance. Discovery of a split infinitive gives some readers a feeling of justification for rejecting a written proposition *in toto*. Breaking a grammatical tradition is more conspicuous than observance of it. Grammar should not become notable by its absence. Correctness is far more, in any event, than a status symbol. Grammatical structure is a means to clarity and precision of sense.

Outrage, as well as applause, greeted the publication in 1961 of *Webster's Third New International Dictionary of the English Language* because the editor described rather than prescribed the use of words in their grammatical relationships. Not only literary journals like *The Atlantic Monthly* and *The Saturday Review* but also *Life* and less sophisticated periodicals protested at the refusal to prescribe a correct usage. Words like "confabbing" and "passel," labeled in the previous edition as "dialectal" and "colloquial," were not so labeled in the *Third*. The editor replied to his critics that he had no "mission" to perform; that his purpose was rather "to find out what educated people are doing with the language"; that, in his opinion, "correctness rests on usage."

The desire to rely upon a dictionary as the quick and easy authority is natural, all the more so in a time of flux. The language, like other forms of human behavior, has undergone cataclysmic changes in the twentieth century. Word choice, like pronunciation, is for some a symbol of status. What the editor of the *Third* did, however, was to throw people on their own as to language policy, to decline the mantle of authority his critics would wish upon him: "Accuracy," he commented, "requires a dictionary to state meanings in which words are in fact used; not to give editorial opinions on what their meanings should be."

"But," rejoined a critic in *The American Bar Association Journal,* "many arguments occurring in the profession of law have been settled by resort to a good dictionary." The task which the *Third* transfers to individuals is to force them to decide for themselves what words they wish to use and in what connection they wish to use them. Businessmen have less of a problem in deciding because the scope or situation surrounding their writing is itself prescribed. Except in advertising, business generally follows tradition. The language likely to accomplish the purposes of business accordingly is more traditional than experimental. Its words are well established, nonambiguous, unpretentious. Sentences are complete and compact. Paragraphs are unified and balanced. In matters where the dictionary does not supply the answer as to what is acceptable usage, the writer must make up his own mind. He can do so the more easily if he thinks of his reader, his subject, his objective.

Whether you support the descriptive or the prescriptive treatment of the language in a dictionary, you must recognize that English now is not the same as Chaucer's English. Once the element of mobility is accepted, you must determine the direction in which you want your own language to move. Dictionary or no dictionary, labels or no labels, you are still the master of your own words. Few writers of the distinction of Henry James have expressed an attitude as practical and pointed as his. His pronouncement, delivered in pure Jamesian style at the turn of the century to a class of girl graduates, is neither dated nor misdirected for executives nowadays:

> The question is whether it be not either no language at all, or only a very poor one, if it have not in it to respond, from its core, to the constant appeal of time, perpetually demanding new tricks, new experiments,

> new amusements of it: so to respond without losing its characteristic balance. The answer to that is, a hundred times, "Yes," assuredly, so long as the conservative interest, which should always predominate, remains, equally, the constant quality; remains an embodied, constituted, inexpugnable thing. The conservative interest is really as indispensable for the institution of speech as for the institution of matrimony.

On occasion, the traditional rules may be honored more in the breach than in the observance. For instance, certain traffic safety posters in New York City caused repercussions when they showed "Tweets," the familiar cat, saying: "That light's gonna change."

"I might ask whether our children are to imitate their instructors," wrote one offended citizen, ". . . or the printed word that is repeated at every street corner?" From the mayor's office came the explanation that the intention behind the posters was to attract the pedestrian's attention and so save his life "at the expense of the reputation of our cats as strict grammarians." The answer to the objections of the grammatically minded correspondent lay in the situation and the intended reader. The same explanation holds for Tom Sawyer's talk. Grammar, like style as a whole, is a matter for adaptation.

Though the advertising profession has taken many liberties with accepted rules, George Gribbin, as president of Young & Rubicam, Inc., charges that ad men go too far. In his words, they "regularly misuse, flagellate, and even profane the chief tool of our trade—language." Among the instances he cites is the use of the adjective "real" as an adverb, "real good." Such a breaking down of distinctions between parts of speech he traces to the natural speech of dirt farmers, cowhands, circus roustabouts, and itinerant fruit farmers, not to professional people. "Have we," he asks his own coworkers, "really become hicks, or do we just want others to think we are?"

Affectation of the role of the common man, of ordinariness in downgrading word patterns, is worth thinking about in understanding our nation's image of itself. The tendency on the part of American business to talk down to the consumer has been as noticeable as the tendency abroad to talk up. It is the contention of the Young & Rubicam spokesman that

> a lot of educated consumers live in this country. Also a lot of clients who not only went to college but often read things of higher literary value than sales figures or each other's annual reports. . . .

He advocates a use of words that observes the rules of correctness.

A further decision about the matter of correctness awaits the young man or woman who joins a long-established company, proud of its record, and jealous to preserve its known reputation. Fresh out of the university, well read, up to the minute in his or her cultural tastes, such a staff member often has a distinct flair for writing, a nonconformist style perhaps. It has happened that such individuals, and older ones too, are novelists and poets on the side. The decision, then, has to be: how to write when doing it in the name of the company? Tried and true forms and style are in standard use. These, if they are what works for the best interests of that company, will be of controlling influence on the writing of the newcomer. Innovation works less successfully than adaptation in most such instances. The question need not be whether to be an organization writer or an individual. What an individual has of skill and artistry in language usage can be added, provided the proven values of the company's written output are not thrown overboard.

When a businessman has worked out a language policy around the principles of acceptability, accuracy, clarity, conciseness, freshness, and correctness, he will have at his command a flexible and serviceable instrument. Such an instrument will be useful to thoughtful people in their everyday affairs, public and private. Thinking and writing are inseparable.

8: Making Communications Talk

When you write a report or a letter, what reaches the recipient? You? Your smile? Your agreeable voice? Your friendly handclasp? No. All that reaches him is a piece of paper with words written on it.

To be sure, if he knows you personally the impact of that piece of paper probably will be affected by that knowledge. Your letter itself will add to or subtract from his total picture of you.

If, on the contrary, he doesn't know you, has never seen you or even talked with you on the telephone, all he has is the piece of paper. That's all: black words on a white page.

When you sit down to talk across your desk, you are inevitably all there, on exhibit, maybe on trial, from the color of your necktie to the timbre of your voice. Anything which you think has not been adequately conveyed by your choice of words can be supplemented by your handclasp, your smile, your gesture, the eye meeting eye.

There are those who blossom over the telephone, feeling a protection for their awkwardness, shyness, or other suspected shortcomings. The telephone instrument affords a sense of control over a situation, a sense of unthreatened privacy where the look in the eye, the set of the jaw, will not be subjected to scrutiny.

All that you appear to be in the personal interview, judged three dimensionally, or all that you sound like on the telephone is, however, stripped away from you when you have to put your business on paper. Do you become a different person, assuming an ink-and-paper disguise? Whether your message becomes a stilted, half-hearted communication depends upon how much of yourself you can impart to your written or dictated word.

Slips Twixt Pen and Lip

Writing, telephoning, and person-to-person talking are three media of individual communication as distinct from mass communication in business transactions. The ease with which they are employed is apt to run in reverse order to this listing of them. You may become a different person in each medium, but if you do it is because you are blocking your true self somewhere along the line. And more often it is the written rather than the spoken word that has a barrier in front of it.

Your personality either comes through your technique of writing or it doesn't. You may be a friendly, modest, natural human being, but if your letter sounds curt, pompous, or obsequious, that is where your business ends.

To learn set formulas prescribed for writing different kinds of business letters is easy, but to make your tone ring true is something that cannot be done by any simple prescription. The run of any morning's mail as it comes across your desk is probably neither offensive nor impressive, merely matter-of-fact and rather toneless. If, when you come to send your replies, you succeed in injecting a touch of yourself instead of letting a sheet of paper with some typed lines on it do all the talking for you, you are sending out something no one else can match.

For tone comes from whatever your communications reveal of your own personality, whatever they show of your relationship to your reader in human terms. Your letter tone is like the sound of your voice behind your spoken words.

The Ring in Your Tone

Some businessmen who are really warm, considerate persons send memos and letters that are terse, cold, cut-and-dried. Some messages that sound defensive, accusatory, and negative are written by people who, if they were face to face with the recipient, would be cooperative, understanding, and constructive. As one engineer commented: "The major problem in my writing is tone. Whenever I'm writing I get the feeling that a stranger is setting down the words. My written language is not the same as my spoken language."

Why this common paradox? Why the unhelpful difference between the written and the spoken word? Simply because the use of typewriter, pen, or dictaphone is allowed to deny the instinct to be natural and direct.

Behind the word barrier a letter writer may strike a tone completely unlike his real self. This may be because he is not "at home" in using the written word, free and easy as he is in meeting his customer, his client, his employer, or his employee person to person. A great deal of comfort has been found in the old myth that some people can write and some simply cannot. That, in business communication, is a myth. Another mistaken notion accounts for some letters that get into the mails: the notion that it is safe to say on paper what one would never dream of saying in person, either of a derogatory or a fulsome nature.

A sense of impunity is assumed by some writers that is as false as the anonymity assumed by the irate and unbridled automobile driver. Words and emotions are unleashed that, if the consequences had to be reckoned with immediately, would never be vented. Because you are putting in writing what you have to say does not mean you can get away with something you would never attempt by word of mouth.

Tone and Technique

If you make yourself visualize the person to whom you are sending your letter, you pick up a tone that is natural, like your word of mouth. Try reading aloud what you have written. Would you be saying it that way if you were actually looking at the person whom you are addressing? And what can you hear him saying in reply? A letter is a two-way process, for usually it is either your answer or your request for an answer. Conversations are dialogues, not monologues, the difference being that in a letter-dialogue the exchange of messages is via the hand and the eye as the written word is transmitted, rather than via the mouth and the ear.

Imagination lies behind the simplest written communication—imagination as to how the other party about to hear from you by mail is feeling, what he hopes to hear, his mood, or state of mind. You as the writer, by placing yourself in his shoes, can meet him part way.

The moment of imagination required to reverse your role as writer to that of recipient is as valuable as the time taken for deciding on the gist of your answer before you set pen to paper, reach for the dictaphone, or buzz for your secretary. The tone you take is as essential as the ring of your voice over the phone or the clasp of your hand in the office.

No technique of letter writing can drown out the tone of a business communication. In sending a difficult "No" reply, such as refusing a customer's request for adjustment, declining a speaking engagement, or terminating credit, you may start in proper technical style by striking common ground; you may then adduce the logical reasons for your refusal and proceed to some counterproposal; you may wind up with an off-the-subject ending replete with best wishes. But if you have masked the sincere and friendly human being that is yourself, the recipient of your letter is going to feel he has been let down.

Technique that smacks of the calculated reaction conveys to the reader a lack of respect for his powers of comprehension. Being frank, even when taking an opposite line, is more of a tribute to his sensibilities than any technical tricks of the trade to make "No" sound like "Yes."

Letters under Pressure

"My delay in replying to you is because my desk is piled high." What, when you see that, is your reaction? Or how about this? "You will understand when I tell you I was called out of the city." Into American business letters there is creeping the recurrent tone of pressure. To the quotations here could be appended "et cetera—ad nauseam." The recipient of a pressured letter is less likely to be struck with the writer's business or importance than with his inability to attend to the matter in hand. The more real and inevitable the pressure is, the more it requires offsetting in tone of voice and in the steadiness of the hand behind the pen.

Factual explanations of business delays are one thing. Piling up of personal excuses is another. Pressure, transmitted to paper, rarely produces the desired results from the reader. If you have to write in haste, and at times who does not, there are technical aids. You can, in giving instructions that will be quick to read as well as write, use the imperative mood of the verb: "Start the new control measures next week." If you want a less hasty tone, try: "You should start the new control measures next week." For something still more persuasive or suggestive, employ the subjunctive or conditional mood: "It would be possible for you to start the new control measures next week." The subjunctive mood requires a caution as far as its usefulness in business goes: it conveys an "iffy" tone, a mood of hesitation.

Consider the tone your reader will be readiest to accept. If he has been waiting for an overdue answer from you, peremptoriness is no better than apology. It is the expectation of receiving no less than the most careful consideration, and perhaps even individual recognition, that leads someone to write you in the first place. If the pressures are such that form letters have to be resorted to, do not be surprised if your correspondent holds the reply up to the light to look for any words he thinks may have been dubbed into blank spaces. This is the ego-impulse at work, which cannot be discounted in business any more than in other circles.

Truly Yours?

Talking through a difficult letter or memo before dictating it, in addition to thinking it through, brings to life the human relations that are involved. Talking, too, frees you of the strange dialect that once cloaked business letters: "Your humble servant," "I am, kind sir," and "Yours of the 29th ult. to hand." Unless you write an antique script with a quill pen, wear high-button shoes, and use a hook telephone, such verbiage does not convey your real tone. Most American business letters, being devoid of the old Victorian formalism, contain the essence of the national character. The new techniques have kicked over the traces of traditionalism and substituted a free-flowing, highly personalized approach.

So it is your own tone that has to do for you on paper what you can do for yourself by deliberate intonation, by the unhurried gesture and glance, in conversation. So technique is merely what other letter writers once found worked best for them. And they had to find out by trying different approaches. Time will never outlast the need for originality, which is itself one technique.

Being original in writing comes down to being yourself, since every writer is an original and not a carbon copy of some other writer. American business, being based on personal initiative, has not accepted the stylized, Old-World decorum of the epistolary art, but is instead developing its own characteristics. The technical message of the American business communication can be put across in a human, persuasive, effective manner by personalized, friendly, and imaginative writing.

9: Saying Yes, No, or Maybe

On-the-job writing, unlike some kinds of writing, is specifically motivated writing. Two motivations are usually involved, both accepted factors in American life: profit and goodwill.

Although a good communication never holds out a grasping hand, the element of gain is, directly or indirectly, at the bottom of it. Frank recognition of this enables you to work from this as your tacit assumption without letting it tower over you or your reader.

Even more basic is the desire for goodwill among people. Business is not different from other walks of life when it comes to human relations. Whereas the unhappy millionaire is a stock character in American fiction, Horatio Alger's boy representing profit plus humanity is the happy hero. So, in writing on-the-job, you find that the profit motivation may play second fiddle to the establishing or reestablishing of mutual confidence between yourself and the person to whom you are writing.

In each message the precise approach to fulfilling this double motivation depends upon the business in hand, of course. What you find on your desk in the form of incoming mail naturally dictates the nature of the reply.

Three Master Patterns

Whether you own oil wells or sell tickets, you may receive in one mail an order for your product, a complaint concerning it, or an inquiry about doing business with you. And there are three master patterns from which to cut the cloth of your reply, depending on the answer you want to send.

You can say "Yes." You can say "No." Or you can say "Maybe." Just decide—that's essential before starting—and you will find your approach ready-made if, that is, your decision is clear at the start.

Yes

How do you say "Yes"? That is the easiest thing, in writing as it is in person. Everyone likes to hear "Yes"; so it can be said directly, quickly, in the first sentence without leaving any doubt about it. If, for instance, you get a letter at the box office asking for a block of seats at the opening performance of a new play, by all means sell the seats. Do it in the opening sentence so that the eager theatergoer is assured at once that he is in time. If, again, you are asked to make a speech which can be fitted into your schedule nicely, by all means let your would-be host know you will come without beating around the bush of self-importance first; without telling him how rushed you are, how many other bids you have had to turn down.

Saying "Yes" immediately isn't, of course, all that has to be done. Once you have given your reader the assurance he wants, spell out the necessary details about time, place, payment—anything else that, if overlooked now, might entail follow-up (and expensive) correspondence.

And one more thing. Why throw away a mutually advantageous situation like an affirmative interchange? Follow up your "Yes" with a word at the close indicating the pleasure involved. Cement the agreeable relation. The "Yes" message is the kind you like to write and to receive. It enables you to open a door and you want to open it fast and open it wide.

No

Saying "No," though harder, is sometimes better to do in writing than in person because you can plan your approach. This may be considered as a different pattern in correspondence or in report writing.

Whenever you have to make an undesired answer to anyone (for instance, turning down a claim for adjustment or declining an interview), think of the other fellow's feelings, not your own. There are times when the shock treatment works—the forthright thrust of a hard and fast "No"; but such times are rare in the average work week.

People do not like to get "No" for an answer, and a negative reply, unavoidable though it may be, puts a strain on goodwill. But saying "Yes" when the situation dictates the opposite might mean throwing out of the window justifiable profit and often, in the long run, the goodwill and respect of the fair-minded individual.

Be sure that you have put your finger on the "No" factor; that you have identified the negative element in the situation. To do so is not always as easy as it sounds. For example, if you have been asked for a report in a week's time but cannot possibly get all the data together in less than two weeks, you have a "No" factor to handle.

In agreeing to prepare what's been requested of you, cope with the matter of time needed, yet avoid sounding as if you will never get it done. Translate, as if from a foreign language into English, a negative aspect into the positive whenever you can genuinely find a positive aspect. Usually, a positive aspect can be found, provided you round the corner and bring it into sight. But refrain from superficial or misleading use of the positive answer.

The human intake for bad news is smaller than a person's intake when he is going to hear what he wants to hear. In handling a negative situation, start slowly, without hitting your reader between the eyes. You need to establish common ground with him. About that report, for example, what can you agree upon with him? Well, there's no doubt that it will need to be based on ample data, though getting the data will take time—up to two weeks, in fact—to compile. There is a difference between being frank and blunt, between tactfulness and abruptness. Disappointing news is better broken when the ground has been laid for it. Would you reply: "I can't see my way to getting this thing finished in weeks, the way my schedule looks"? Look at things again, now: "In two weeks' time, I can have the report ready with the specific facts you need."

Having found some area where your minds meet, proceed to explain the whole situation. If you are able to get your reader to follow your reasoning, going logically step by step with you, he may arrive at the "No" answer before you have to spell it out for him. A business relationship that is adequately explained permits the reader to draw his own conclusions, even if the conclusions have to be in the negative, so that you are not held to blame for whatever is contrary to the reader's wishes.

A way out can customarily be discovered so that "No" need not be forever. Given some ingenuity and thoughtfulness, you can put your finger on a possible alternative. Although you have to say "No" to a specific claim, your explanation will do more than protect the profit angle. It can also salvage goodwill, without which there will never be another time. A door can be shut without being slammed.

Maybe

The third test of successful response is posed by the kind of communication that contains a possibility but not a certainty, neither "Yes" nor "No," but a letter where the situation is essentially "Maybe." Maybe you will get agreement to what you are writing; maybe you will make a sale; maybe you will get your terms accepted.

You need from the official of a neighboring city certain information concerning industrial sites. Or you are inviting the regional conference of tax consultants to meet in your city. Frequently, you have to enlist support for your product. All this may be called drumming up trade.

The person to whom you write in such "Maybe" situations will have to be persuaded. In persuasion, there is more room for experimentation in the reactions to be stimulated than in the situation calling for a flat "Yes" or "No" answer. Some "Maybe" propositions are more persuasive when presented head on, quickly and to the point. On the whole a carefully selected avenue of approach often produces better results.

Look at the map; spot where you are going with your message; plot the best route to your destination. If you can point out how the situation may interest or benefit your reader, that is one way to start. No one is above self-interest, whether in the broad or the narrow sense. You have to supply, or at least indicate, the incentive in your "Maybe" situation. Whatever avenue you choose, you will not get far if you point out at the end of it only what you want or need from the reader. What is in it for him, the person you are seeking to persuade? Can you make him want to go along with you?

Having started on the right road leading to the reader's advantage as well as your own, take time to tell your story well. If, in your opening paragraph, the mayor of the big city gets the idea that your industry is the kind his city wants, tell him next about your projected plant. He will not miss the point, even though you use the device of suspense. You may want to indicate that you are just making initial inquiries regarding future location, and that other mayors are sending you information also about their sites.

In the matter of persuasion, you have plenty of room to experiment. Not only do the "Maybe" situations differ, as between selling an automobile or inviting a speaker to your organization, but readers differ in their reactions. So the comeback or the kickback (as the case may be) depends upon your intuition and creativeness.

Just remember that the point you make last should be the best one, because it is what you leave uppermost in your reader's mind. In a quick way, the approach patterns that have been suggested for the three basic letter situations—the affirmative, the negative, and the persuasive—can be tested. Let us consider their applicability in the regular communications of a retailing business. Among its key departments may be personnel, sales, credit, adjustment, public relations. After noting these divisions, consider the flow of letters by some of the subjects most commonly handled by them. We can now try to apply to the writing of such letters the three overall approaches:

Types of Business Letters

		Yes	No	Maybe
Personnel	Applications:			
	(for jobs)			x
	References:			
	noncommittal	x	x	x
	unfavorable		x	x
	favorable	x		
	Offers			x
	Acceptances	x		
	Rejections		x	
Sales	Orders			x
	Acknowledgments:			
	filling	x		
	declining		x	
	back-ordering			x
	substituting			x
	Sales:			
	initial			x
	follow-up	x		
Credit	Credit:			
	application			x
	recommendation	x	x	x
	inquiry	x		
	grant	x		
	refusal		x	
	Collection:			
	bill (invoice)	x		
	reminder	x		
	inquiry			x
	appeal			x
	ultimatum		x	
Adjustment	Claims			x
	Adjustments:			
	granting	x		
	refusing		x	
	compromising			x

Types of Business Letters (continued)

		Yes	No	Maybe
Public Relations	Goodwill	x		
	Inquiries			x
	Replies:			
	accepting	x		
	declining		x	

Once the letter writer determines in his own mind whether his message is basically affirmative, negative, or persuasive, the letter is partially composed. He has, in other words, determined what the emphasis is to be. Now all he has to do in outlining his message is to use knowingly the positions of emphasis at the beginning and end.

Why Take Pains in Writing?

Why, when all is said and written, should we take pains to win Dear Reader? Why bother about how to say "Yes" clearly and completely, how to say "No" painlessly, how to turn "Maybe" to account?

You need to care because business cares about what the other fellow thinks, even more about what he feels. American business has to care because the man in the street, the man on America's Main Street, the common man if you like, is king. He does business where, when, how, and with whom he likes and no one else. This is the private side of private enterprise. Reader reaction counts.

Appendix

Sentence Building for Variety

The variety of sentence patterns available to writers is wide. The basic structural patterns are customarily described as simple, compound, and complex. Here is a little story that will show some of the changes you can ring on sentence structure:

A Sad Tale
(with Happy Ending)

At the conference, the assistant gave his report to the President, the author of many reports.

"Mr. President, please accept my report." The President and the Vice-President looked very bored. They picked up the document, leafed through its pages, and seemed surprised. Then they paid the writer and his secretary an unusual compliment. The wording was clear, the material was factual, but they immediately considered the next step. They needed some recommendation which would implement the findings.

"We will promise action if you will spell it out." When the report had been authorized, no recommendation had been specifically requested. Then the solution would have been easier than it would be now. Whatever might be recommended must be worthy of executive action. The two top men listened to what their assistant now suggested.

The recommendation which all three drafted then and there met with general support. The conference ended only when all were tired but happy, the report writer realized. (The End)

To show the particular sentence "mix" involved in composing this episode, diagramming is the easiest way. Diagrams are a graphic way of reviewing the grammatical construction of different kinds of sentences. (Diagramming symbols used here are those from *Studies in Grammar* by M. C. Hermans. New York, 1924. Other grammar books use similar, if not the same, symbols.) What the symbols are used to indicate may first be illustrated for you:

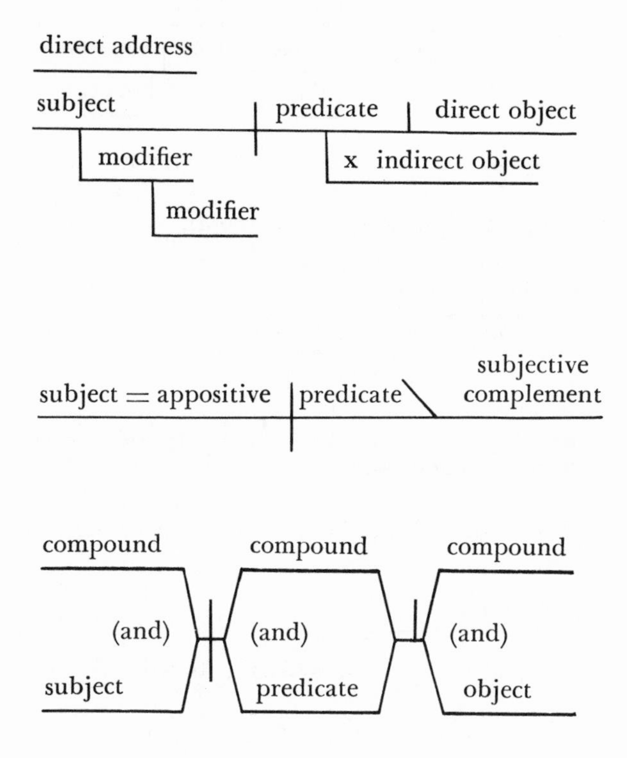

Now here is "A Sad Tale" as it looks in diagram form:

1. At the conference, the assistant gave his report to the President, the author of many reports.

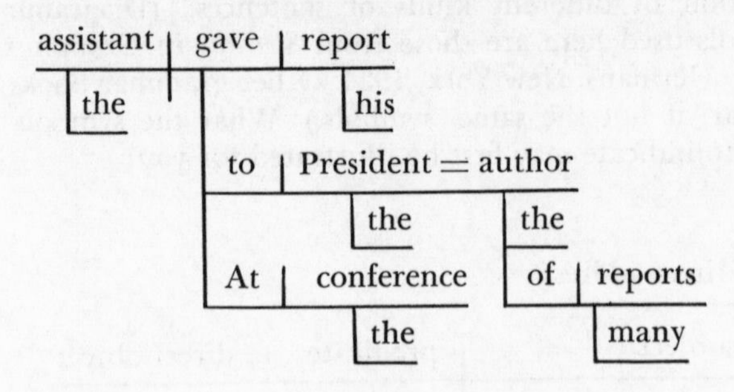

(Simple declarative sentence with an appositive.)

2. "Mr. President, please accept my report."

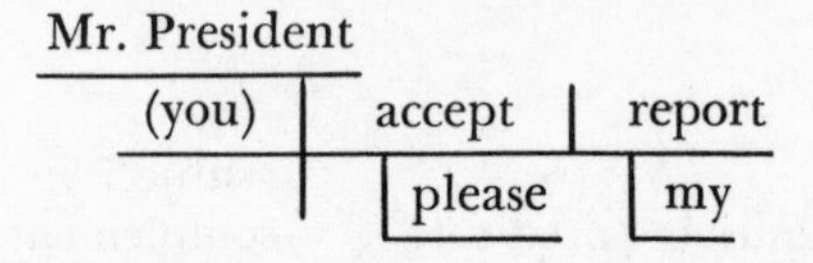

(Simple imperative sentence with understood subject and words in direct address.)

3. The President and the Vice-President looked very bored.

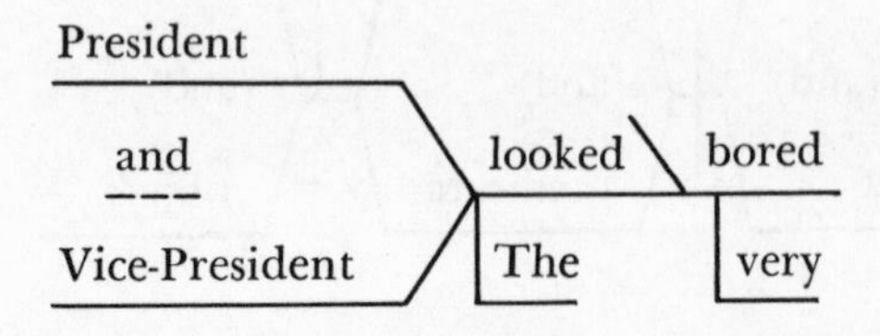

(Simple sentence with compound subject and subjective complement.)

4. They picked up the document, leafed through its pages, and seemed surprised.

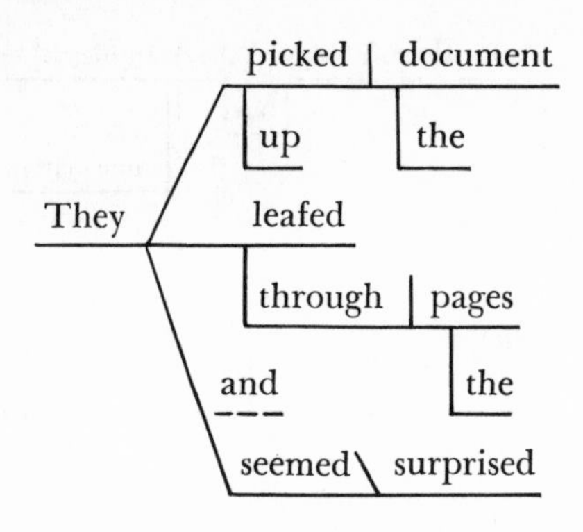

(Simple sentence with compound predicate.)

5. Then they paid the writer and his secretary an unusual compliment.

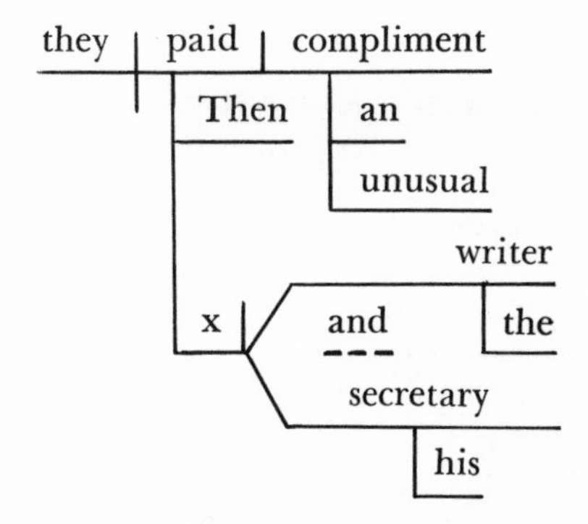

(Simple sentence with compound indirect object of verb.)

6. The wording was clear, the material was factual, but they immediately considered the next step.

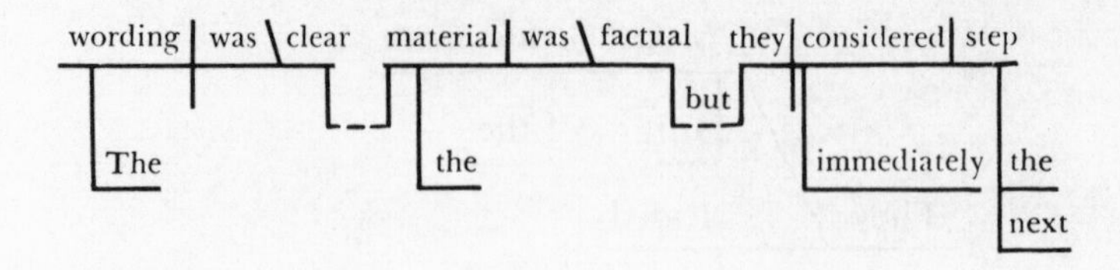

(Compound sentence.)

7. They needed some recommendation which would implement the findings.

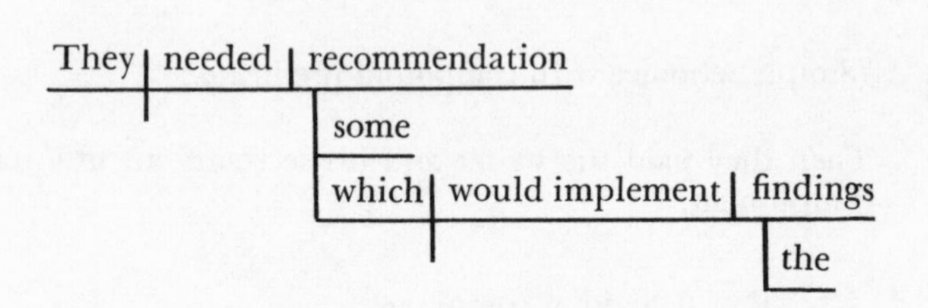

(Complex sentence with adjective clause.)

8. "We will promise action if you will spell it out."

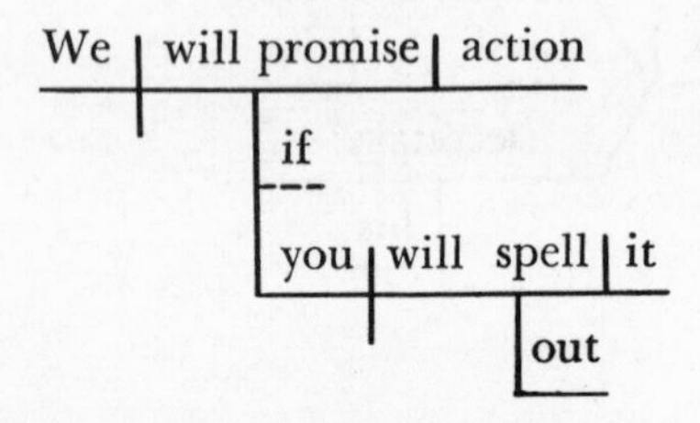

(Complex sentence with adverbial clause using a subordinate conjunction.)

9. When the report had been authorized, no recommendation had been specifically requested.

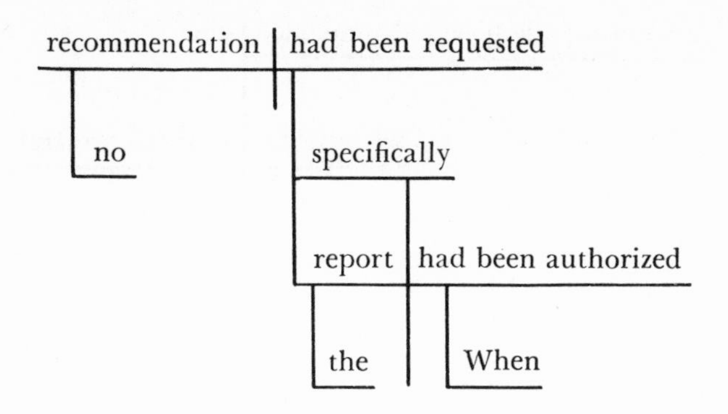

(Complex sentence with adverbial clause.)

10. Then the solution would have been easier than it would be now.

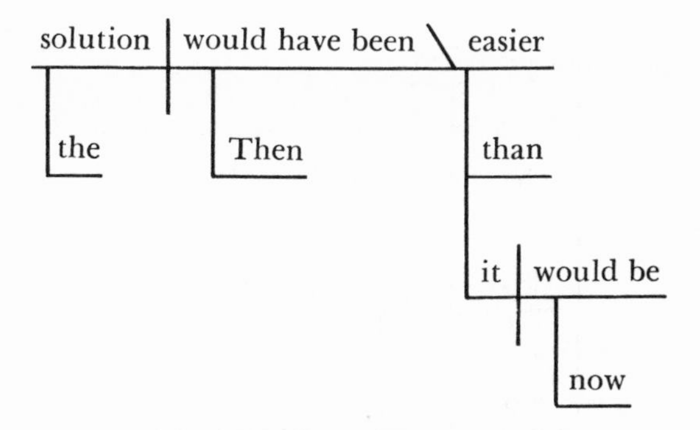

(Complex sentence containing an adverbial clause. [In such comparisons, two of the elements are often not expressed: "Then the solution would have been easier than now."])

11. Whatever might be recommended must be worthy of executive action.

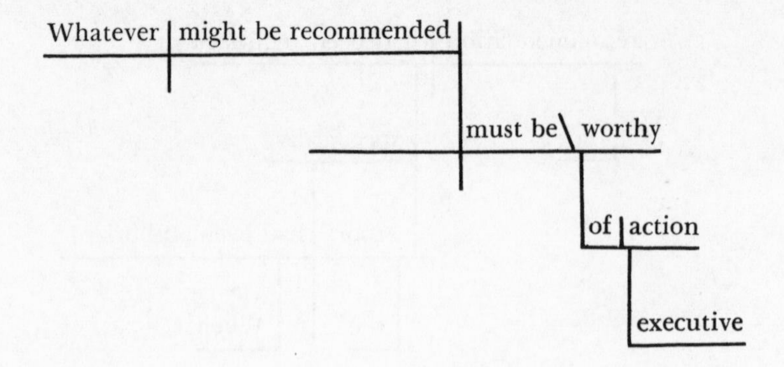

(Complex sentence containing a noun clause as subject.)

12. The two top men listened to what their assistant now suggested.

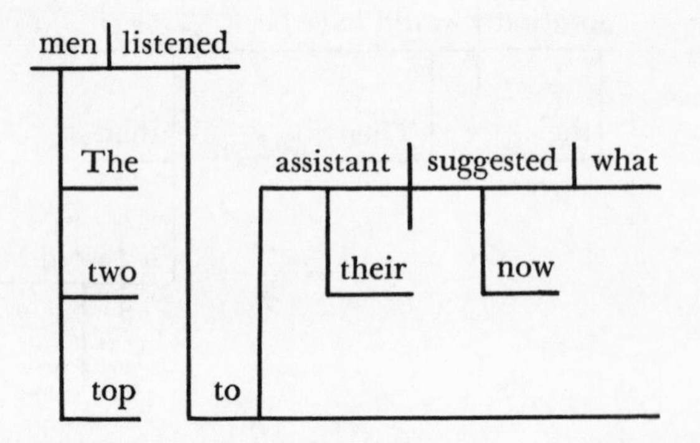

(Complex sentence containing a noun clause as object of a preposition.)

13. The recommendation which all three drafted then and there met with general support.

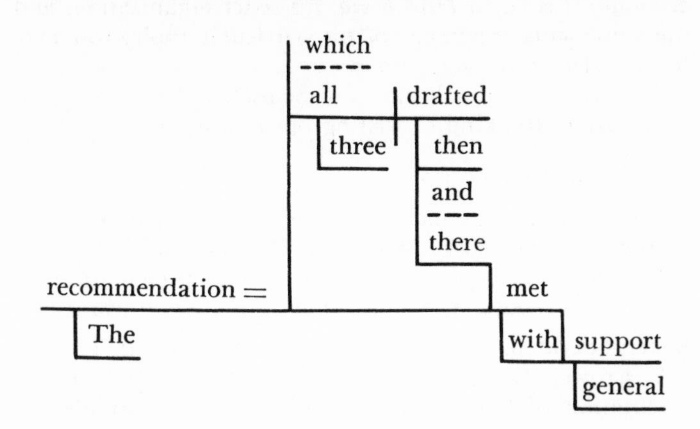

(Complex sentence containing a noun clause in apposition with a noun.)

14. The conference ended only when all were tired but happy, the report-writer realized.

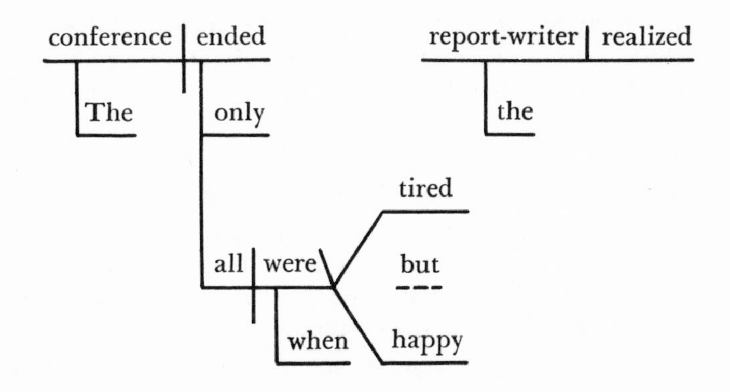

(Complex sentence containing a parenthetical clause.)

Reading Suggestions

If you discover principles you can adopt from John Hersey's economical style in *Hiroshima,* his strict organization, and the convincing treatment of his particular topic, you may like other reading suggestions.

The books listed will show for themselves the relationship they bear to the kind of writing business needs.

Convenient Reference Sources

Anderson, C. R., Saunders, A.G., and Weeks, F. W. *Business Reports.* New York: McGraw-Hill Book Co., Inc., 1957. Excellent textbook. Detailed technical presentation of parts of a report, style, typography, etc. Gives illustrations.

Baker, Sheridan. *The Practical Stylist.* New York: Thomas Y. Crowell Company, 1962, paperback. Compelling presentation of "the natural linguistic facts." Suitable for newcomers and old-timers in the practice of writing.

Bromage, M. C. *Cases in Written Communication.* Ann Arbor: Bureau of Business Research, Graduate School of Business Administration, The University of Michigan, 1964. Compilation of actual problems that have arisen in American firms in which written documents played a part as cause or cure.

Carey, G. V. *Mind the Stop.* London: Cambridge University Press, 1958, paperback. Amusing, informative commentary from the English point of view on punctuation marks —their why's and wherefore's.

Curme, G. O. *English Grammar.* New York: Barnes and Noble, 1957, paperback. Practical for rules.

Fowler, Henry W. *A Dictionary of Modern English Usage.* New York: Oxford University Press, 1965. Words and expressions, alphabetically listed, with interpretation of their accepted meaning and suitability.

Gregg Publishing Division, *20,000 Words.* New York: McGraw Hill, Inc., 1934. A pocket-sized remedy for chronic misspelling.

Hunter, Laura G. *The Language of Audit Reports.* Washington, D. C.: U. S. Government Printing Office, 1957. Detailed and specialized.

Kierzek, J. M., and Gibson, Walker. *The Macmillan Handbook of English.* 4th ed.; New York: The Macmillan Company, 1960. Complete, clear, well-indexed, well-organized reference book on grammar.

Menzel, D. H., Jones, H. J., Boyd, L. G. *Writing a Technical Paper.* New York: McGraw-Hill, Inc., 1961, paperback. Condensed and racily written guide to preparation of a technical manuscript.

New American Roget's College Thesaurus. New York: Signet Books, 1961, paperback. Literally, a "treasure house" of synonyms to help avoid repetitive wording.

Van Piper, Henry, and Davie, Frank E. *Guide to Technical Reports.* New York: Rinehart & Company, 1958, paperback. Condensed booklet describing and illustrating technical set-up of report presentation.

Points of View and Writing

Anderson, W. L., and Stageberg, N. C. *Introductory Readings on Language.* New York: Holt, Rinehart and Winston, Inc., 1962, paperback. Diverse and authoritative contributors.

Bernstein, T. M. *Watch Your Language.* Great Neck, N. Y.: Channel Press, 1958. Practical tips on what to write and what not to write from a top editor.

Davies, M. B. T. "Reporting to Clients on Management Services Engagements," in *Lybrand Journal,* vol. 41, no. 3, 1960. Specific and pertinent for special type of reporting.

Davis, Keith. *What You Should Know About Administrative Communication.* Bloomington, Ind.: Bureau of Business Research, School of Business Administration, Indiana University, March, 1954, pamphlet. Useful summary of factors relating to communication on the job. Theory of the situation, who says what to whom, when, and why.

Davis, R. G. "Logical Fallacies" in Locke, Gibson and Arms, *Toward Liberal Education*. 3rd ed.; New York: Rinehart & Company, 1960. Summary of faulty habits in thinking as they are reflected in words.

Editors, *Fortune*. "The Language of Business," in *Fortune*, November, 1950. Also in Locke, Gibson and Arms, *Toward Liberal Education*. 3rd ed.; New York: Rinehart & Company, 1960. Critical discussion of stereotyped expression and jargon as they occur in business.

Einstein, Albert. "The Common Language of Science," in Einstein, Albert, *Out of My Later Years*. New York: Philosophical Library, 1950. A few profound but simple pages on the precision and clarity possible in scientific communication.

Fielden, John. "What Do You Mean I Can't Write?" in *Harvard Business Review*, May-June, 1964. An inventory of current causes for the unreadability of much office writing.

Gowers, Sir Ernest. *The Complete Plain Words*. London: His Majesty's Stationery Office, 1954. Lucid, reasoned advocacy of established standards. The approach is theoretical yet practical.

Graves, Robert, and Hodge, Alan. *The Reader over My Shoulder*. London: Jonathan Cape, 1947. Plea from a poet for application of human considerations to everyday writing.

Hall, E. T. *The Silent Language*. Garden City, N. Y.: Doubleday & Co., 1959. Exposure of human sensitivities to the impact of words.

Hayakawa, S. I. *Language in Thought and Action*. New York: Harcourt, Brace & Company, 1949. Fascinating discussion of what words mean in the human give and take. Semantics.

Huxley, Aldous. *Words and Their Meanings*. Los Angeles: Anderson and Ritchie, 1940. Essay on language as more of an art than a science. Interesting, of indirect help.

Keyes, Langley Carleton. "Profits in Prose," in *Harvard Business Review,* January-February, 1961. Plea for better writing.

Lambuth, David. *The Golden Book on Writing.* New York: The Viking Press, Inc., 1964. Suggestions, not rules, from a knowing teacher on how to make language work.

Orwell, George. "Politics and the English Language," in Locke, Gibson, and Arms, *Toward Liberal Education.* 3rd ed.; New York: Rinehart & Company, 1960. Acerbic.

Stevenson, Charles L. *Ethics and Language.* New Haven, Conn.: Yale University Press, 1944, paperback, 1960. Profound philosophical analysis of the moral and social implications of what people say and write.

Strunk, William, Jr., and White, E. B. *The Elements of Style.* New York: The Macmillan Company, 1959, paperback or hard covers. A best-seller. Do's and don'ts about writing based on good taste from someone who knows.

Thouless, Robert H. *Straight and Crooked Thinking.* London: Pan Books, 1960, paperback. Exposure of pitfalls in the reasoning process.

Demonstrations of Principles of Writing

Bacon, Francis. *Essays.* Garden City, N. Y.: Dolphin Books, Doubleday & Co., Inc., undated, paperback. Pithy observations of pragmatic value, in style and content, for contemporary affairs.

Hemingway, Ernest. *The Old Man and the Sea.* New York: Charles Scribner's Sons, 1952. Simplicity of style designed to fit subject. Scrupulously organized account.

Hersey, John. *Hiroshima.* New York: Bantam Books, 1959, paperback. Presentation of fact with emotional impact, demonstrating skillful organization, controlled vocabulary. In substance, a report with inferences left up to reader.

Irving, Washington. "Rip Van Winkle," in most collections of Irving's works. Author achieves rapid progression of narrative by means of chronological sequence and citation of factual data.

Plato. *Dialogues.* Any edition. For demonstration of sheer logical analysis of a topic in Socratic discussion. The interplay of information and opinion.

Poe, Edgar Allan. "A Cask of Amontillado," "Descent Into the Maelstrom," in most collections of Poe's stories. Effect of intensive organization in moving reader rapidly toward author's objective.

Wilder, Thornton. *The Bridge of San Luis Rey*. New York: Bonibooks, 1936. Masterpiece, partly due to unity in organization.

Index

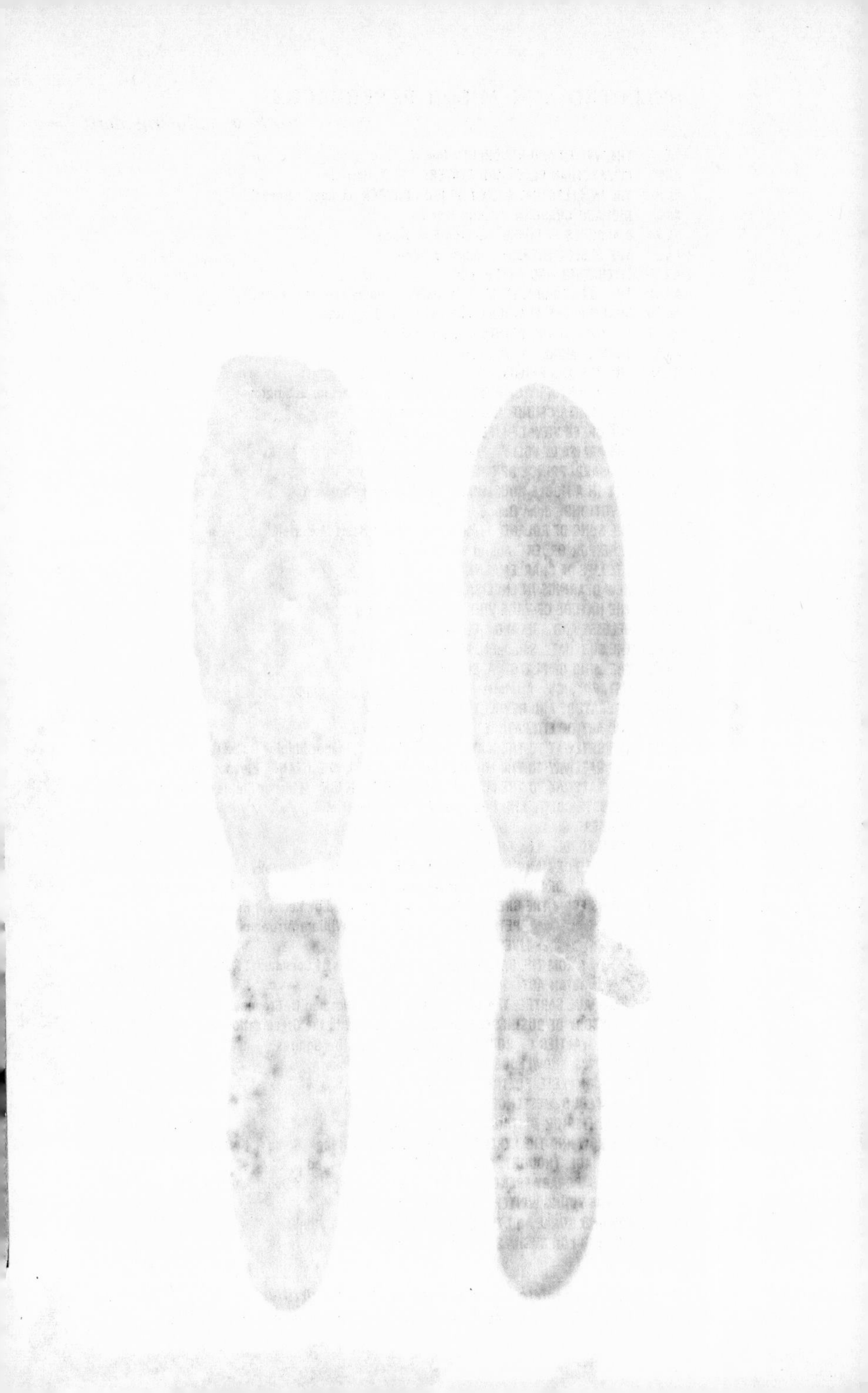